Juliet Erickson is a freela͏ works with politicians, senic entrepreneurs around the world. She has worked with the successful London Olympic Bid Team, and guest lectured at Stanford University and London Business School.

She is also the author of *The Art of Persuasion: how to influence people and get what you want:*

'*A How to Win Friends and Influence People* for the communications age.'

Independent on Sunday

'We all know what we want, and this book will help us get it with a smile.'

You magazine

'Juliet is amazing. She changed the way I look at things completely. I have never experienced anything like it. I know so many people who need what she has to say.'

Henrietta Spink, activist, campaigner and founder of
The Spink Foundation

nine ways to walk *around* a boulder

using communication skills to change your life

juliet erickson

Kyle Cathie Limited

First published in Great Britain in 2008 by
Kyle Cathie Limited
122 Arlington Road
London NW1 7HP
general.enquiries@kyle-cathie.com
www.kylecathie.com

ISBN 978-1-85626-726-7
© 2008 by Juliet Erickson
Design © 2008 by Kyle Cathie Limited

Project editor Caroline Taggart
Design Jane Humphrey
Copy editor Sally Somers
Index Alex Corrin
Production Sha Huxtable

Juliet Erickson is hereby identified as the author
of this work in accordance with Section 77 of the
Copyright, Designs and Patents Act 1988.

A Cataloguing in Publication record for this title
is available from the British Library.

Printed in England
by Cox & Wyman, Reading, Berkshire

this book is dedicated to my mother:
your courage is an inspiration

contents

acknowledgements

My heartfelt thanks go to my dear friends who helped me keep
my eyes on the prize.

Peter Lockyer, for your love and patience.
Anne-Maree Fitzsimons, for helping me keep mind and body
connected.
Kourtney Harper, for being so generous with your curiosity.
Caroline Taggart, my editor, for your good ideas wrapped up in
humour and wisdom.
Sally Somers, for bringing a clever breath of fresh air to the
creative process.
Kyle Cathie, my publisher, for that first meeting and all the fun
that has followed. Thanks for your trust and support.
Borra Garson, my agent, for your pragmatism and guidance.
The sales and publicity team at Kyle Cathie – I am really
grateful for your early attention and enthusiasm.

introduction

We all face personal challenges in our lives, challenges that can seem like boulders – immovable obstructions standing between us and our goals. Often the same old boulders crop up time and again. They are many and varied, and may include:

- anything you have ever said that started with 'I'm not really good at...' or 'I get really stressed at the thought of having to... or 'I wish I could, but it never happens...' or 'That will never happen for me'
- nervousness when facing a roomful of people you don't know
- feeling stuck over how to move forward in your life, your job or your relationship
- an inability to resolve an issue with someone in your life – be it a difficult boss, a stroppy teenager or an elderly parent
- not knowing how to deliver bad news, clear up a misunderstanding or apologise

All too often we react to the boulders in our path by pushing and shoving in the hope of shifting them, even when we know that pushing has never worked. It is worth remembering that, in the wise words of Benjamin Franklin, the definition of insanity is doing the same thing over and over and expecting different results.

For over twenty years, I have been helping some of the world's most successful people to persuade, pitch, negotiate and sell millions of dollars' worth of business. And one thing I have learned is that whether you are the CEO of a major corporation, an entrepreneur or a mum dealing with her teenagers, your personal boulders are essentially the same. Whatever the challenge, in my experience, bad communication skills are eighty per cent responsible for lack of personal success.

Many of my clients believe that they are calling me for a quick fix in a high-stakes moment. As we work together, however, they often come to realise that what they thought was a short-term problem is actually a longer-term issue. The situation that needs fixing or managing in that make-or-break moment nearly always turns out to be what I call their boulder. It is magnified because of the intense pressure of the situation, but more often than not relates to a recurring problem.

Human communication works in mysterious ways. There are so many variables and unknowns at work between people that it is daunting to imagine the odds against us getting it right with each other. Our own level of awareness, and our ability and willingness to communicate, can be thrown into a soup bubbling with the equally complex characteristics of the person across from us. This soup is laced with fears and expectations, bad habits and distractions. For most of us, it is very difficult to extract ourselves and listen to what is going on in the moment we are in. On top of that, it is also difficult to listen to ourselves.

I'm not a psychologist. I don't deal directly with the underlying reasons why someone can or can't, will or won't. And I have found that it's not always important to 'deal' with the root cause, or even to move it out of the way before proceeding. Nor is it always necessary to understand the reasons for something getting in your way, in order to get around it. Sometimes you just need to move on.

In my work, I am often under tremendous pressure to get to the best solution speedily and with the least resistance. I have to move people or teams to a place they never dreamed they could get to in such a short time. That's why I've become an expert at walking around boulders – when the stakes are high and failure isn't an option, you find solutions, and fast.

Now I want to share some of those solutions with you. I want you to see that you can use communication behaviours as a way to release yourself from bad habits that don't serve you, and replace them with new, more useful ones. These habits can be physical, such as shallow breathing in times of stress or tilting your head a certain way. They can involve posture, such as leaning forwards or backwards when you talk, or changes in your speech, so that you don't begin a sentence with, 'I'm sorry to bother you but…' when what you mean is, 'Please get on and do what I have asked you to do.' These may not sound much, but believe me they can make a world of difference. I've learned that no one needs to stay stuck; there are fun, simple and unexpected things we can all use to get the results we're after.

The techniques you will find in this book can be applied to a range of situations – depending on what you need or want and what the best outcome is for everyone concerned. I have practised them with people whom you would least expect to be open to them. I have made intuitive guesses under pressure and experimented in the heat of the moment. I have had the joy of proven experience and watched with pleasure the successes of thousands of people. The results, I offer to you.

So, what can you hope to get from this book? Here are some realistic expectations. You will be able to:

 ▪ understand how your personal communication skills affect your life and your ability to make things happen
 ▪ learn how to change behaviours that may be blocking you from what you want to do or be in life
 ▪ increase your level of awareness and flexibility, and be able to adapt to everyday situations more easily and thoughtfully, making life less stressful
 ▪ use techniques you may not have expected, to bring about lasting positive change in all aspects of your life

I don't believe there is a lot of new news in the world, and this book is no exception. Most of the biggest blocks my clients face are addressed by the same few but timeless solutions. Often when real change occurs, it feels as if you have always known what the solution was – you just haven't recognised it until now.

So, if you're longing for change, willing to take responsibility for your actions and ready for a better and more interesting life – read on.

chapter **one**

when the student is ready, the teacher will come

First of all, I should say that in adopting this old saying I'm not necessarily referring to a teacher in the conventional sense. Rather, that what you need to do or change will happen when you are ready – and *only* when you are ready, no matter how much you are pushed or cajoled by other people. When this time comes, you will do what you need to do with strength and clarity. You will have discipline and direction.

However, Louis Pasteur said that chance favours the prepared mind, so saddle up!

Most people don't really believe they have the power to shape and change their lives. It is not usually until we are adults that we start to become aware of how many of our behaviours and attitudes lead us into destructive or counter-productive habits that hurt us and those around us.

A habit is simply the same decision made over and over again. If you are habitually fearful or anxious, you may not be able to reliably gather information about your environment or the more subtle events going on around you. In order to get more control over these bad habits, you have to be more aware of yourself, and learn to monitor your responses. Think of self-awareness as just another habit. The catch is that it requires you to be honest with yourself and accept responsibility for your personal growth. This in turn gives you more control over your state of mind, your health and your sense of well-being.

If we constantly bump into a boulder, it is primarily because of our ideas, attitudes and belief systems. By belief systems, I don't mean anything to do with religion as such, I mean ingrained ideas that we have about ourselves. Experiences we have – bumping into our boulders again and again – confirm and reinforce our beliefs. Unfortunately, many of our belief systems don't serve us and can be harmful to our well-being and peace of mind. So if we believe that we are not clever enough to succeed at something, whenever we fail we reinforce our lack of faith in our ability to succeed. By bumping into our boulders, we give life to these beliefs about ourselves, regardless of whether they are useful or not.

There is another kind of ingrained belief that affects our success. I like to call it 'the bikini diet'. Unfortunately, it is a widespread problem that has to do with wanting the results but not wanting to put in the hard work. On the one hand, there are the bikini dieters who dream of being able to wear a bikini, and who buy the magazines, torture themselves mentally, but do nothing about it. On the other hand are the people who want to get away with wearing a bikini but have no such long-term plans for getting to that point – they want instant results, a magic quick fix. A friend of mine once said that 'you can fake it for fifteen minutes'. For many this might seem good enough, but it's only a matter of time before you are rumbled.

 case study The bikini diet: wanting the results without the hard work...

The only thing wrong with being a bikini dieter is that it can become a habit, and one where you think you are doing something, when in fact you are doing nothing. It is okay not to be ready. Don't rush into anything if you aren't sure that you have the right level of commitment yet. Be mindful of kidding yourself with a bikini diet.

There are two categories of bikini dieters: the Panicker and the Soaker.

The Panicker calls me at the last minute in a mild stew about not having enough time to prepare for an important make-or-break moment. In order to accommodate them, I must drop everything and come immediately. In the past, this has meant flying to far-flung places, working late into the night, making stressful and risky eleventh-hour changes at much greater cost than if we had thought about them earlier. The truth is, the Panicker has known about the problem well in advance but for some reason has waited until there is almost not enough time left to do what needs to be done. In a sense, they are secretly sabotaging the enterprise. These circumstances call for numerous compromises, and there is no time to make real changes; it's almost like stepping into an emotional war zone. The real work never gets done.

I recently worked with my favourite Panicker, a long-standing client called Martin, on a very important speech he had to make at a gala charity event. Many of his peers would be in the audience and he had discovered that it might be televised. Panic. Could I come immediately, as it was happening in two days. I rearranged my schedule and Martin's secretary sprang into action and flew me from London to his office in Hong Kong, for what was going to have to be a 24-hour turnaround. The speech hadn't even been written, much less rehearsed. I knew Martin had a mortal fear of public speaking and would do anything to get out of it. He avoided it with a passion, even though he was a high-profile person who frequently put himself in the spotlight.

So I wrote the first draft of the speech on the plane, and we worked the following day with a mock-up podium in his office. When the time came for me to leave, he was still nervous and looking for a way out of doing it.

The key here is that I could tell you the same story more than ten times about working with this same man over the years. It is as if each time is the first time. He only wants the solution that gets him through his fifteen minutes.

The Soaker is the person who earnestly and diligently takes an interest in getting around their boulders, works very hard, has clear objectives for personal growth but doesn't do anything about it. Soakers soak in the information and insights about what they can do to help themselves, but don't take the first steps. They attend the appointments, do the courses, study. They just don't change anything.

People in the coaching professions need occasionally to stop working with a client who is not committed or ready for change. It is an ethical issue: can you continue to add any value to this person? If not, you shouldn't be taking their money.

I had to say goodbye to a client recently because for six months he kept finding reasons for continuing our sessions, but then not carrying out the actions we agreed upon. Graham was attentive in the sessions, but by the time we met again there were always excuses about why he didn't get round to the hard work. He initially asked for help after a performance review that identified a number of areas in his communication skills he needed to improve. He was told that if he didn't improve certain things by his next review, he was unlikely to be promoted. So our sessions were organised around his clearly stated objectives. Each time we met we talked about his progress since the last session. And each time he said he 'hadn't had a chance to get to it but had another issue he wanted to talk about'. He wanted to discuss something new he had faced, or asked if I knew of a particular course or book reference, or for my point of view on some related communication subject. He kept skirting around what we had agreed.

By our third or fourth session, I confronted Graham about this issue and he said he thought our discussions were helping him. He promised to try the exercises we had decided on. By the next session he still hadn't 'got round' to it. I asked if he needed us to involve his peers or his manager – sometimes this helps reinforce the new behaviours and support the person in their environment. I told him I found our discussions interesting, but I would need to stop seeing him if he couldn't adhere to the brief we had agreed. He said he would think about it and call me when he was ready to start work.

He didn't call back and recently I heard he was working with another coach who had been signed up for an indefinite period. He was not promoted at the next review and to my knowledge still sees his 'adviser' each month.

The Panicker and the Soaker share a common characteristic. They are not ready to face their boulders, so they do what they think is enough. The problem is that, in my experience, most of them keep repeating this behaviour pattern and find it difficult to break out of it. Panic or soak, they are easy options.

Although I believe that anyone can learn to change these bad habits, there are limits to how much reading a book can help. No matter how skilled or aware you become, some situations are unlikely to improve. If the people involved in your life are emotionally troubled, the stakes extremely high or the history very intense, you might not be able to improve the situation, however hard you try. Importantly, the timing may be wrong. However, what you can do to improve the likelihood of getting through remains the same, regardless of the context. For every difficult situation that is genuinely insurmountable, there are many more that look that way and are not.

I can say with my hand on my heart that communication holds a crucial key to transforming our lives. I am committed to helping you with your momentum, energy, and determination to move forward in your life – when you are ready.

By buying this book you have already taken that first step towards changing something. But first steps don't take you very far if you don't keep on walking. I once had a long-term client who spent a fortune on self-help books (that he regularly and generously donated to the local charity shop after reading them). I like to think of him as having his engine in neutral. Always running and ready to engage, but never leaving the parking-lot.

Some people wait for a heart attack or divorce before making necessary changes to their lives. It seems to me that this means they spend far too much time in situations that make them unhappy or unfulfilled. Better, surely, to reach that moment of your own volition.

So, how can you let the 'teacher' know you are ready? Here are three things that I believe you can do to help yourself along:

- Take the focus off yourself.
- Aspire to get it right most of the time, not all of the time.
- Trust that you already have what you need in order to achieve your aims.

Take the focus off yourself

What would you think if I told you that the best way to truly, madly, deeply change the way you are is to take the focus off yourself? That to develop and improve, you should shift your focus on to others? The self will flourish if you remove it from under the microscope. Sounds counter-intuitive, doesn't it? But remember that your perception of what is going on around you, good and bad, right and wrong, is only ever, at best, half the story. I'm not ignoring the importance of knowing thyself. I don't mean you to sacrifice your needs and desires – just to put them into perspective. Since knowing thyself is a lifetime pursuit anyway, you may as well balance your effort by putting as much or more attention on those around you right now. Doing so gives you a more accurate reading on the everyday. Your world relies on how others respond to you. This is something over which you have more control and influence than you probably imagine.

It is true that it is more difficult to understand others before you more clearly understand yourself. However, the reverse is also true. You can fine-tune your understanding of yourself by focusing on others. Find opportunities to practise objectivity, compassion and neutrality. There is a lot to be gained by seeking first to understand before being understood.

Aspire to get it right most of the time, not all of the time

Getting it right most of the time is worth the effort. I have had many clients who have been in therapy for years and who still beat themselves up because they procrastinate about the next step, stay in that job they hate, take their health for granted or continue in a relationship they don't enjoy. All the therapy in the world does not make them any easier on themselves, because they are striving for something completely unrealistic – they are aiming to be perfect, fault-free people who get it right all of the time. Face it, you will get it wrong sometimes – that's just the nature of the human condition.

My experience tells me that striving to get it right all of the time brings nothing but trouble and disappointment. Worse still, it takes you down a narrow path of doing only what you think you can do well. Being human, most of us have an overinflated idea of how well we do many things, but our attempts at perfection are just that – attempts. We can, and do, achieve glorious excellence, but rarely perfection.

People who seek perfection live in a restricted world of self-deception. I find these types the most difficult to work with, because while they may seem high achievers on the surface, if you dig a little deeper you find they lack the skills or will to adapt to change. They are the ones who drop out of high-stakes situations at the last minute, who prepare till they are exhausted and then revert to their comfort zone when you need them most. They have sound excuses for doing it 'their way'. They have their 'groove' and they think it is right just the way it is.

Thinking we should get it right all of the time leaves the road littered with casualties. The truth is, the best of us only get it right most of the time. The gap between the world as it is and the world as we want it to be causes so much stress in life. Cut yourself some slack. Have a sense of humour about what life throws at you. Sometimes things get so awful that all you can do is laugh at the absurdity of it all.

Trust that you already have what you need in order to achieve what it is you want to be or do

The trick here is to have faith in your own being, to know that you are complete and ready. Throughout our lives, most of us are not encouraged to understand or develop our intuition or feelings. The more you learn to listen to your inner self and follow it, the more you will trust that it will bring what is best for you. You may have been ten years in a job you no longer enjoy. You ask yourself quietly and the answer from your inner self is, 'Leave the job, you are unhappy, you are not growing, find something else.' Then your rational brain kicks in and says, 'No, you need the money, how will you pay the bills, do you really have something else to do?' Yet every time you ask the

question you get the same response: 'Leave the job, leave the
job…' Eventually you will need to make a decision and you will
hopefully do it with the right balance of facts and inner
guidance. Until you try and test your inner guidance you can't
learn to have faith in it. Only then will you be able to act in a
different way. It is difficult to trust that you can and will make
the right choices for yourself, no matter what, or that what you
want will come your way – particularly if you have spent a
lifetime telling yourself otherwise.

The key lies in your own self-awareness. Put simply, you
have to start to pay attention to what you are doing. Sometimes
it only takes small, focused experiments with postures or
mannerisms to generate the beginning of new actions and ways
of thinking. Many of the techniques I will recommend to you
might seem simple, or may involve nothing more than making
minor changes in your movement or speech. Some of my
recommendations come from my tested variations on the
Alexander technique, the Feldenkrais method, Pilates, yoga, tai
chi and meditation. What they have in common is that they are
slow, gentle, nurturing methods that bring your energy inwards
rather than scattering it. Essentially, they teach you how to be
quiet and to deliberate, so that you can listen to yourself. This
can help you go past just the physical and lead you towards
understanding more about your mind and your heart.

Remember, it doesn't matter why you do what you do or why
you feel a particular fear – what matters is that certain habits
may be blocking you from having an easier, less stressful life.

While it isn't always important to 'deal' with or understand
the underlying reasons, attitudes or self-limiting beliefs before
tackling them, such an approach can help you to become aware
of how your belief system might be causing you to feel low
self-esteem, fear or mistrust. If it is, you need to consider

replacing it with more positive ideas of self-acceptance, encouragement and trust. I have recommended an exercise below that may help you.

A word of caution. Identifying self-limiting beliefs is important, but it can also become self-limiting in and of itself. Endless agonising over the origin of a bad attitude can be just as bad as the attitude itself. Don't blame your parents or your upbringing for something you can't kick. Remember that bad habits are bad decisions made over and over again. If you create them, you can also get rid of them. You have the power to do this – in fact you are the only one who can.

An exercise: self-limiting beliefs and awareness in your body

I like this exercise because it helps you become more aware of how your physical body speaks to you when your boulder is reinforced by your attitude. It is recognised amongst coaches and practitioners and there are a number of variations.

Find a quiet place where you won't be disturbed. You can do this exercise with a trusted partner or friend if you wish.

On a piece of paper, write down the beginning of a sentence, 'A negative thought I have about myself is...' and finish the sentence with whatever comes to mind. Don't think for too long – do it quickly and with as many sentences as you can think of.

Be aware of how you feel as you compile the list. How are you breathing, what are your physical sensations?

When you have finished, read the sentences out loud and mark the three or four that upset you the most. Notice if your breathing is getting difficult, your throat is dry, if you have cold hands, feel tension in the back, shoulders, stomach, neck or hands, or sensations of anger or sadness.

Then find the one most disturbing sentence – the most limiting belief you have about yourself. Write this out again at the top of a new page and reflect on thoughts and memories associated with what you have written.

Then write about how this negative belief has affected your behaviour and self-expression throughout your life. When does it affect you most?

Now, we are going to experience how your body feels about this belief.

Repeat the words of your most self-limiting belief, aloud or silently. At the same time, adopt the posture that corresponds to how you feel when you read it. For example, you may find that you want to sit on the floor with your arms wrapped around your knees or stand firmly upright with your arms crossed. One of my clients described her self-limiting belief as making her posture look as though she was about to be struck by something – shoulders up tight near her ears, knees bent and hands clasped. Allow your body to find the posture of your belief and note your breathing, sensations and impressions in your body as a whole, and where in your body you feel the most tense.

When you have found the posture that feels 'right', stay in it for several minutes and repeat the words of the self-limiting belief you wrote on the page. Continue to pay attention to how you feel, accepting as much as possible the different emotions and memories that come and go.

After some minutes, release yourself from the posture, shake off the accumulated tension in your body by walking around the room, stretching and moving until you feel relaxed again.

Now that you have identified your most self-limiting belief, you must pay attention to how it functions in your life. Be aware of how it expresses itself and observe your behaviour in various situations. If you find yourself in situations where you are behaving according to this belief, consciously choose to believe a different idea about yourself, and notice how the atmosphere changes. Observe the link between your physical posture and your inner thoughts, and use that connection to affect change. When you move differently, you think differently, and vice versa.

You can help yourself by becoming more aware of the underlying belief systems that create habits that don't serve you or those around you.

The idea that 'when the student is ready the teacher will come' applies to us all, and we all beckon the teacher in different ways. The three ways I have highlighted above – taking the focus off yourself, aspiring to get it right only most of the time, and trusting that you already have what you need to do it – will make it easier for you to notice when the time is right, and to proceed with the right state of mind.

chapter **two**

fix the physical

The premise of this chapter is based on the old saying that actions speak louder than words. I've always wondered where this came from – other than my grandmother – and it turns out it first appeared in 1652 in a pamphlet called *Will and Doom* by an American doctor and pastor called Gershom Bulkeley. You learn something new every day...

The role your physical body, behaviour and actions play in making change easier or harder for you is a formidable force for individual change. Actions speak louder than words is a crucial driver behind your ability to move on.

Observing yourself

Whenever you decide to change an ingrained habit, the part of you that created it is likely to resist your efforts. These habits are hard to shift – they have become embedded as a survival tactic, and they may seem to be part of your identity. A client once mentioned that she felt everyone loved her bubbly personality and her sincere offer of 'my door is always open'. She had been this way for years at home and at work. It wasn't until she found herself exhausted from working long hours and from frequently having a houseful of visitors ('strays', she called them), that she realised that in always saying yes to people she had handed over control of her time and her privacy.

Every year she vowed to learn to say no more often, and for years it didn't work. The same applied for a workaholic friend determined to get to the top of his field, who was absent for most of his children's toddler years. I know he felt bad and it caused a lot of trouble with his partner, his kids and his health, but still it continued.

Sometimes you might really struggle with change despite your best efforts: psychologists acknowledge this and refer to it as 'reversal' – trying hard at one thing and ending up doing the opposite. You start to get negative and self-judgemental. When you decide you want to 'be more assertive' or 'exercise more', 'work less' or 'eat more healthy food', you lose confidence when you don't follow through. The more you try, the more you fail, and so on in the cycle.

The habit you want to change comes from somewhere in your experience – your upbringing, culture, things that happened to you or even things that happened to someone you know. These are powerful influences that you may or may not be aware of. But I don't think in every case it matters if you know where it came from or even that you must necessarily 'get over it' psychologically before moving on. Sometimes accepting it and taking action is enough.

Here's the fascinating thing. Scientists tell us that our habits set up a muscle memory in our brains – in effect, a storage place for elements of our mental state. Associated with that are all the unnecessary tensions and stress factors that we accumulate and experience. So, in effect, our habits and their tensions, both good and bad, stay 'stored' in our physical bodies. If you know what to look for and are prepared to see, you can observe them. And in observing them, you can start to change them.

If you want to minimise or eliminate these unnecessary tensions, the beginning step is most certainly to acknowledge that they are there. You need to acknowledge that you have a behaviour that is not serving you.

I believe that the key to change lies in the very moment before you start to engage in the habit. If you can retrain your 'memory' by suspending your usual response, you allow yourself to make a better choice.

I refer to this delicious suspension of response as your moment of truth. Imagine a moment of truth as that instant – usually a few seconds or even milliseconds – before you 'do' the thing you want to change. This instant is characterised by replacing the old behaviour with a new one. You make a choice that is more consistent with what you really want.

As you become more aware of how to create your moments of truth, the habit you want to kick becomes something that is not going to limit you any more. You create time to replace the behaviour. You walk around the boulder.

Let's begin at the beginning. Recognising your habits and changing them begins with understanding your own patterns of behaviour.

Medicine, both ancient and modern, categorises our body types, and how we typically behave, as a guide to understanding the human condition and providing a framework for diagnosis and cure. I think this is particularly relevant to us today, as lay people, because we can use observed behaviour as a starting point for learning to help ourselves and others.

Think of a set of behaviours that could be considered 'typical' of the way you behave. All of us have a fairly predictable set of behaviours that are, say, how you act most of the time without thinking about it. They might include things that people closest to you would say if they were asked to describe you. These typical behaviours come naturally to you, and shape how others perceive you, the impressions you create. They relate to the type of person you do or don't get along with, and affect your degree of comfort with change or confrontation, the level of emotion you use in your decision-making, stress levels and attention span, amongst many other things.

These typical behaviours are your default mechanism – something that happens automatically unless you actively override it. We all have a default type that is predominant and that will come across most often. This is important because the default can also influence what sort of habits you may develop.

Being aware of these defaults will help you not only to become more able to make the most of your own strengths and weaknesses, but also to devise your own strategies for walking around your boulders and moving on.

Most common default types

I categorise these according to whether you:
- command and control
- rationalise, employ logic and order
- get friendly and seek harmony
- feel it and say it

As you look over these types, you may recognise yourself. I will show you some of the most common blocks each default type brings with it. Through this you may recognise types you get on with better than others, or pick up some tips on how to adapt your behaviour if you are interested in improving a relationship. In each of the default examples I have chosen what constitutes, in my experience, the most difficult hurdle for each type.

Command and control
If this is your default type, it is likely that you:
- prefer an environment that is tidy and organised
- can come across as impatient, glancing at your watch or interrupting
- use little or no small talk – you cut to the chase
- prefer people to be specific when they are explaining something – you don't like them to tell stories or take too long

- use questions and answers that are short and to the point
- don't mind an argument or confrontation
- are usually forceful or energetic
- watch the time closely and are interested in reducing time spent on things
- like to control agendas and conversations
- respond well to order and punctuality
- may appear calm in tense situations
- are well structured in your thinking and verbal expression

Your default behaviour stems from being comfortable when in control, and from a desire to get to the point. You may have been told that your directness can be intimidating and possibly perceived as inaccessible or controlling. Others may find it hard to express their true feelings to you. 'It takes a while to get to know you' is a common response to this default – not necessarily because you want to remain inaccessible or to keep people away, but because your behaviour has an energetic quality of confidence in terms of 'telling' people things. Being definite. Knowing the answers. It is almost a kind of 'pushing' – pushed for time, pushing for a result.

Physically, people who use this default behaviour tend to hold their weight slightly forward when they are standing or seated. Their eye contact is usually strong while speaking and listening. They don't gesticulate much and, when they do, it is to make a point. They tend to make statements rather than ask questions. Their facial expressions are limited. Their voices are usually strong and clear.

case study Tina: a question of tactics

The most difficult hurdle for the Command and Control type is adapting to and building relationships with their opposite default style – the Get Friendly and Seek Harmony type.

I am thinking of Tina – a friend who is a retired military officer. When she retired, she decided to use her extra time and skills to help the charity sector. This was a generous offer, of course, because she had many good financial and organisational skills to contribute. Her husband quietly invited me to dinner one night at their house because after weeks of interviewing for various volunteer positions she wasn't having any success. What was happening? Her time wasn't costing anything – she couldn't give her services away!

I wish you could have been sitting around the table to see her face as she described the various people she had met and what had happened in the interviews. She was bewildered. She said she had sent ahead an agenda by email to each person, along with some of the questions she would like to ask (so they could prepare). She then called to confirm before the meeting, and kept to time, having completed the objectives of the meeting. Wasn't that the right message to be sending to people in a sector struggling to make ends meet?

If you are familiar with the volunteer/charity sector you know it is run mostly by people with big hearts and a genuine concern for those less fortunate than themselves. They are a sensitive bunch who often care more about caring than about efficiency for efficiency's sake. I could see Tina was in 'tell' mode even before she got to the meetings. Her robust, direct style, which was well structured and objective-driven, made her kind offers feel more like commands.

I advised Tina to try a different strategy and new tactics (the right language to use with her!). Based on her understanding of the people she would like to work with, I suggested she adjust her style to suit them, so they would feel more like she understood them, and that they could work with her.

Her overall strategy now became to build a relationship with the people she was talking to, and to help them feel comfortable during the interview. We practised how the next conversation might go, starting with some relaxed and relevant small talk. We sorted out what she knew about the next interviewer and what she needed to find out beforehand in order to personalise the meeting and carry on a different conversation. She could now talk about some subject (which may have included the interests of the other person) other than her CV or her goals, and how well she understood the goals of the charity.

So that she didn't feel completely lost, we built a clear structure around a few important questions rather than statements. Questions that gave the interviewer a chance to elaborate rather than just answering yes or no. By organising the time, using questions around issues in order to explore them, she was able to present her credentials as well as learn. For example, having discovered through her homework that an important issue concerned the charity's lack of success at fund-raising that year, she constructed a conversation that began by asking about how they raised funds, instead of launching into a lecture on how to build a fix-it campaign. Or, knowing she was short-listed with two other candidates, she devised a question to help her understand how they would be making their decision. Instead of talking at length about her qualifications, she asked, 'What will be the most important criteria you consider when making your decision...?'

The meetings then became more like a personal conversation than an interrogation. They would think, 'Now, at last, here is someone I could work with!'

Tina tried this approach and found it a really useful way to achieve her objectives. She worked hard at adjusting. I met her again some weeks later and she told me that she 'practised' with her husband before she left for meetings. Before long, she had accepted a position with a well-known hospice.

The key change for Tina was replacing the 'telling' and 'pushing' behaviour with new 'asking' and 'listening' behaviour. She prepared questions before the meetings with the intention of creating a tone of cooperation and calm. She resisted sending an agenda ahead of time, and gathered more personal information about the interviewer so she could understand their motivations and interests better. She relaxed in her chair rather than sitting forwards throughout the whole conversation. She talked less and listened more.

Rationalise, employ logic and order

If this is your default type, it is likely that you:

- have a home or office that is tidy and organised
- are on time for gatherings and meetings
- are logical and fact-oriented
- will often ask for detail
- are the one who reads the instruction manuals
- respond to questions with unimaginative, precise or qualified answers
- enjoy technical challenges
- have a low-key tone and manner with minimal facial expression
- are proud of being thorough or exhaustive
- will make decisions only after you have all the facts
- will take the extra time if needed to 'cover all the bases'
- are not comfortable with confrontation

This default stems from a preference for order and sequence, and a discomfort with confrontational situations. You tend to express yourself in a fairly low-key way, often making your feelings 'hard to read'. Sometimes this impression of being low-key can be interpreted as slow to act, stubborn or set in your ways. Perhaps this is because this default response is often to reject decisions or actions that rely largely on intuitive judgements (not enough detail) or avoiding the feeling of being rushed or pushed.

Physically, people who use this default behaviour often carry their weight evenly balanced on both feet, shoulders rounded or relaxed, head slightly forward. They tend to sit back and deep in their chairs, arms in their lap or folded across their body.

 case study Daryl: information overload

The most difficult hurdle for the Rationalise default style comes in adapting to and building relationships with their opposite default style, the Feel it and Say It type.

The most archetypical person I have met with this default was a man called Daryl. Daryl's boss asked me if I would take on the task of helping him to prepare for a very important presentation for a meeting with his company board. He had been unsuccessful in the last presentation meeting, and he had one more chance to get it right. He was given feedback that the meeting got bogged down in detail, ran over time and went down an irrelevant cul-de-sac.

When we first met up, I began by having him explain a little about his audience and their expectations. I learned that the board was made up of six people, each known for their flamboyance or creativity in their chosen field. They tended to change subjects mid-meeting and often did not stick to the proposed agenda. As we discussed this, and how he might handle it, he suddenly became very uncomfortable and wanted to stay focused on the content and detail of his message. Here was the core of the problem. He believed that more was better and that if the content was good enough and in a logical order, he would be fine.

My plan was to show him how he could have some structure and order, but at the same time give the tricky audience a sense that he was willing and able to wander off track. The key lay in starting to control the process early on. The more information and insight he could have before the meeting, the better. This would mean less surprise (which the Rationalise types like to avoid) and more opportunity for flexibility (which Rationalise types are not naturally good at). We began by coming up with questions to ask some of the audience (those who would talk to us) in the week before the meeting, to help Daryl set an objective and tailor his content. The biggest benefit, however, was that by being in touch with the board members beforehand and asking about their areas of interest, he was feeding their egos and building individual relationships with each one, outside the very raucous and out-of-control group context. The questions were:

- What are the key issues that concern you most?
- Which of those are the most important?
- Why are they the most important?
- What would block (or promote) your support?

Together we met face to face or had phone conversations (with his boss's blessing) with as many of the board members as possible, in order to get their views. This worked wonders for Daryl, who was astonished by the outcome. The meeting was a success. His level of nervousness, as well as his subject matter, changed completely. He was more relaxed and less rigid in his approach.

Daryl learned that his tendency to rely on content and structure meant he had not been focusing on the people or the outcome. As a consequence, his communication was too long, too detailed and missed the mark. He now begins his preparation by gathering information about and insight into the people he needs to inform or convince. He takes this opportunity to start to build a relationship with members of his audience, and as a result understands both what needs to be done and the tone in which to do it. He doesn't start writing content until he is sure of what he must achieve and for whom. Giving presentations is never going to be his favourite activity, but with a little bit of pre-work of the right kind he is starting to experience some success in what are for him the most difficult circumstances.

Get friendly and seek harmony

If this is your default type, it is likely that you:
- enjoy being around people
- find it easy to make small talk
- like to know how other people feel before making decisions
- avoid confronting others
- have lots of personal items on display in your home or office
- don't find it easy to argue in the moment, but may go away and seethe
- are proud of relationships and friends
- are considered warm, patient and supportive
- share personal experience easily

This default behaviour stems from a desire to seek consensus and harmony. Because of this, you may appear to be lacking confidence or assertiveness in some situations where you should stand up for yourself. You are generally known to be fair, quick to defend others and trusted with confidences, which makes you an easy and friendly colleague.

Physically, people who use this default behaviour usually

have expressive faces and create empathy and comfort by 'mirroring' their postures with others. They build rapport and connect with people easily and naturally.

 case study **David: Mr Nice Guy**

The most difficult hurdle for the Get Friendly types is adapting to and building relationships with their opposite default style, Command and Control types.

David is a popular person at work and in his community. I had dealings with him on a client project years ago, then recently he called to ask if I would meet him for lunch to discuss a position he had accepted as chairman of his son's school board.

In the lead-up to our meeting, I remembered one of David's real skills as a team member on our previous project. There were many people from different bodies involved, all with vastly different agendas. His kindness and cheerful attitude kept us positive during long hours, late nights and tight deadlines. He was always available to listen to problems, came up with suggestions for solutions, and pulled the team together – a wonderful facilitator.

After we had caught up on the news of each other's lives, we came to talk about his new role as school board chairman. I could see him physically tense up as he described the last few meetings. By the time he had finished talking about it he had gone from relaxed and chatty to irritable and stressed. What was going on?

In his role as chairman, he was called upon not only to listen to problems and complaints and to facilitate solutions, but also to make unpopular decisions. It was the reality of needing to do this that was making him uncomfortable. He disliked it so much that he was procrastinating over certain decisions and making the other board members angry. The qualities for which he was known and admired were now the cause of his grief. He was facing a situation where he needed to be more direct and commanding or he was going to be ousted.

He felt that resigning was not an option, so we developed a strategy for moving forward, allowing him to attack his problem in a credible and courageous way. The solution was to play to his strengths as a consensus builder, and present to the board a mandate to ultra-formalise a more democratic approach to decision-making. He would still listen to and consider all points of view, but would facilitate a solution with the group, and put the propositions to the committee to vote for the final outcome. He needed to be seen to make a decision. Now, a decision to approach decision-making more democratically! Of course!

He was able to manage more confidently by adopting this approach (which included the possibility of being democratically voted out of the job). A week or so later, I heard that the board had accepted his idea.

Feel it and say it

If this is your default type, it is likely that you:

- exist within a slightly disorganised environment
- enjoy creative challenges
- like positive personal small talk
- dislike detail
- are excitable, articulate and animated
- enjoy hearing about personal achievements
- can be judgemental
- consider pride and ego to be very important

The most common challenges for the people who have this default stem from a weakness for distractions and a tendency to take things personally. I have often seen people of this type running into trouble because of the force of their personality (for which read ego).

Physically, Feel it and Say it types tend to be energetic, gesticulate a lot, move easily and speak quickly.

 case study Megan: leaping before you look

The most difficult hurdle for the Feel it and Say it type is adapting to and building relationships with their opposite default style – the Rationalise type. A Feel it and Say it type's natural creative and spontaneous approach can run into trouble when they have to deal with their opposite style, who naturally distrust their enthusiasm. They can risk losing credibility, and they then feel they have to claw it back by proving themselves twice over.

After her second child, my neighbour Megan decided she wanted to set up her own playgroup. She could imagine that over time both her children (eighteen months apart) would play with other children their age in a fun and safe environment. She also saw this as a way to meet other parents and make some new friends. She and her husband had just finished building an extension to their house, and the new spare room would be a perfect place for the children to play.

That same day she discussed it with her husband and decided on the date and time for the first group. A short letter went out to parents and friends.

The response was fantastic. In just the first week, over seventeen parents confirmed that they would come. By the day of the playgroup, twenty-three parents had accepted.

Any of you who have ever been involved in a playgroup know what I am about to say. It was a disaster. There were 23 parents, and 31 children ranging in age from six months to nine years. The parents were shocked, the children were fighting and making a mess, and Megan was shattered.

Megan's enthusiasm for the big idea, in tandem with her expressive style, meant she hadn't thought to do the homework. She was keen to be the first playgroup in her neighbourhood and was motivated by the positive response. The more support she got, the harder it was for her to see the need for detail – such as what sort of behaviour was acceptable and how would it be handled? What notice would be required if a child was not able to attend? Could substitutes take the place of an absent child? Would visitors be invited? Who would provide toys? Were any foods off-limits and were there any allergies? Who would be responsible for cleaning up? Oh my. See what I mean?

I had a coffee with Megan a few days later, and we discussed the nightmare that was her good idea. She told me she didn't want to give up on it, but was lost as to how to win people back in order to make it a success. Playgroups were a widely accepted form of entertainment for children, so there was plenty of advice around. She hadn't sought any of it. Time to begin again.

Simple things like a set of written guidelines could have saved Megan a lot of trouble. Two key strokes on the internet and a chat to a woman at the local council, and she was on her way again.

I helped her re-write the letter to only a few parents with children of the same age as hers (one of the important criteria), with a set of questions to be discussed at a pre-meeting and agreed before a playgroup could start.

As a result of the pre-meeting with the selected parents, it was decided that one of the other mothers would help out with the organising, while Megan could get on with finding new members in nearby neighbourhoods. She acknowledged her tendency to 'leap before she looked' and she made a commitment to herself and her family to prepare more effectively. She told me that she has introduced a cooling-off period before she acts on an idea. She has taken to writing the idea down and pinning it on the fridge so she can look at it for a while. Along with this, she has decided not to commit herself so easily to new things. Her new motto is: 'If I can't make a case for it on paper, I won't do it.' Slowing herself down has helped her focus her enthusiasm only on the projects she has taken time to think through.

As for the playgroup, I have since seen much smaller groups of happy people walking in and out of her house on a regular basis.

Of course you are not strictly only one of these default types. You'll probably find that you have characteristics from a combination of two. This is not about putting anyone in a 'box', but in my experience, there are certainly observable behaviours and preferences we all have that can give us insights into how to change habits that may not be serving us.

Observing others

You can also use the insight in this chapter to help you to build better relationships with people whose default types are opposite to yours. Consider the people whom you find it most difficult to relate to naturally. If you default to Rationalise, you may find the Feel it and Say it type difficult to relate to. If you are a Get Friendly you might find Command and Control intimidating. You can use behaviours to build a bridge and connect to someone who is not like you, by behaving more like they do. This is a concept known as mirroring. It is happening on one level when we instinctively match the pose and gestures of another when we feel at ease with them. By being consciously aware of it you can use it to build subtle connections with people. For example:

If you want to build a better relationship with a person who defaults to Rationalise:

- Be on time for meetings or social engagements.
- Don't rush them, take your time.
- During discussions, make sure you have some facts or evidence to back up what you are saying.
- Don't use soft words like intuitive, gut feeling, believe, feel, etc.
- Instead, use words such as know, prove, demonstrate, analyse, etc.
- Don't exaggerate or use sweeping statements.
- Be low key in your style, careful, thoughtful and not too enthusiastic or perky.
- Don't answer questions too quickly or interrupt.

If you want to build a better relationship with a person who defaults to Command and Control:

- Be on time for meetings or social engagements.
- Don't linger too long after the party is over.
- Make your stories and jokes punchy.
- Be up on current events and refer to them as examples.
- In conversation try making your point first, then explain the detail.
- Don't think out loud.
- Avoid rambling.
- Make any letters to them short and to the point.
- Answer their questions in a brief and specific way.

If you want to build a better relationship with a person who defaults to Get Friendly:

- Be late to meetings and social gatherings if you need to, but have a good personal reason.

- Be warm, friendly and talkative.
- Ask about their family.
- Don't rush them. Do things at a relaxed pace.
- Show you are interested in how others feel.
- Send thank-you notes.
- Talk about your personal experience where relevant.
- Get together for reasons other than business.

If you want to build a better relationship with a person who defaults to Feel It and Say It:

- Be on time for social and business gatherings.
- Try to appear confident and dynamic.
- Be creative and colourful – explore ideas.
- Keep the detail to a minimum.
- Don't compete.
- Keep up with what the other person is saying.
- Be spontaneous – suggest something different.

Recognising the behaviour you don't want, and replacing it

So now what do you do? It is very difficult to recognise your own bad behaviour – you are so close to it that you can't see it. Unless someone points it out specifically or gives you some clue, it is not obvious to you. Replacing bad behaviour adds another layer of complexity. Let's have a look at a powerful way to help you understand your own behaviour, which may give you some insight into how you can help yourself.

Each person mentioned above had one thing in common. In order to change their behaviour, they applied a technique that would help them become more aware of how they felt just before they bumped into a boulder. Remember earlier I said that the key to changing lies just in the moment before you start to engage in the habit. If you can retrain your 'memory' by suspending your usual response, you allow yourself to make a better choice. Here is how the technique works.

Your task is to pause whatever you are doing a few times per day, for a few minutes, to note how you are feeling and what you are doing. Where are the tensions, head to toe (if any)? Take a helicopter view of how you are standing or sitting. Where are your hands/feet, how are you breathing, how is the tension in your head, shoulders, back, facial muscles? I know a few minutes is a long time – if you need to start with one minute, do it. Aspire to three. As you become more skilled in personal awareness, stopping before you bump into a boulder will become more natural and easier for you.

Tina, the Command and Control ex-military charity worker, learned that as she prepared for her meetings, and during them, her spine was tight and erect and her jaw was clenched. She sat forwards in her chair, leaning in towards the other person. This behaviour was accompanied by her using direct statements and 'commands', and her voice was slightly louder than the person across from her. By paying attention to this she replaced the behaviour with a softer posture – a more relaxed spine, sitting back further in her chair and softening her facial muscles and her hands. She also mentioned that crossing her legs made a difference to her, improving her ability to listen.

Daryl, our Rationaliser, found that he was rounding his shoulders, looked down at his paper while speaking even when there was nothing on it, and tended to speak very quietly in front of a room full of people. He also didn't make much eye contact while speaking. As he became more aware, he learned that his new style of preparation (focusing more on the audience) made eye contact easier and more frequent. He sat more upright and his voice became clearer and easier to hear. He was given feedback that he was more 'definite'.

David, our Get Friendly chairman, noticed that he was very expressive in his face – always smiling and exaggerating affable expressions. His face was tired by the end of the day and there was a lot of tension in his shoulders and back. He also noticed that he responded positively and too quickly to what people were saying. His shoulders and chest were open and almost thrown 'back', making him feel somehow off balance. Learning to tone down his facial expressions and easy affirmations, and listen silently instead, removed a lot of tension in his face and neck. He also found that standing with his shoulders relaxed and breathing deeply more often relaxed his back.

Megan, our Feel it and Say it mother of two, realised that when she was on the verge of committing to a new idea, she was nearly always standing, shallow breathing, talking quickly and gesticulating. Her voice was louder than usual and she moved quickly from place to place while telling others about it. She learned to put a barrier up – time – between this behaviour and a decision. She now sits, breathes, writes it down and waits.

I'm not going to pretend that this is easy. Stopping yourself doing what seems to come 'naturally' – but is really a habit you may have built up over a period of years – can be incredibly hard at first. But I have worked with many people using this approach, and have seen marvellous results. By persisting, you create the habit of observation. By creating the pause that gives you time to think about what you are doing, you can choose a different behaviour.

If the idea appeals to you, consider supporting your moment of pause and awareness with an affirmation. Combining change in physical behaviour with the appropriate language can be used with reasonable success. Said quietly or aloud (it depends on what works for you or whether you are at home alone, on a crowded train or in a restaurant), these words are also wonderful as a focus for your meditation. Here are a few I have found and recommended to clients, but it is equally valid to create something that works for you. Sometimes your pause will reveal its own special affirmation!

- I am calm in this moment – I will only think of the one thing I am doing.
- I want to feel good and I trust that I will put my energy where it needs to be.
- I know there are others who have been where I am now and have found a way that works for them.
- This is all good and everything will work out just the way it is supposed to.
- Even though I have this......I deeply love and accept myself.

Be sure that your affirmation does just that – affirm. Watch your language so that no negatives creep in. A growing body of evidence in the study of psychology shows that people who have a positive attitude are more effective in the world, more successful, stay healthier and heal more quickly than people who are negative in their outlook.

Fixing the physical means that you can use signals from your body to recognise, understand and change habits that may be getting in your way. It isn't easy, and requires both patience and a commitment to supporting yourself through the process. Be nice to yourself, cheer yourself on, give yourself time and space to learn. I know you can do it.

chapter **three**

getting the
message across

On my first date with my partner several years ago, he did something I have never let him forget (lovingly, of course). The electricity was buzzing between us over a quick glass of champagne at the bar, glittering meaningless small talk and laughter. We were called to the table for dinner, we sat down and were handed our menus. The silence was tantalising. After a short pause of glancing over the menu, he made eye contact with me and asked, 'So, what is your book about?'

I can still see it happening in slow motion – a second later, as I opened my mouth to answer, he dropped eye contact and went back to reading the menu. I was aghast. Why did he ask me such an important question if he wasn't going to attend to the answer? This was our first date – wasn't he supposed to be interested in what I was doing? How rude, how unaware. And so on. I don't remember my answer, or if I even gave a proper one. I can only remember how long it took me to recover from the initial distraction.

Our relationship survived, but what happened between us that night is a good example of how easy it is to mess up your intended meaning.

Prepare, deliver, make sure…or else

When you are face to face with someone, the structure of your communication is divided into three distinct parts: prepare, deliver and make sure. These three parts act as the connective tissue of your total message or impression. They are there, like it or not. They complete each other. You can't have effective communication if they stand alone or are in the wrong order.

The sequence prepare, deliver, make sure, means you need to pay attention to:

▪ how you prepare someone to receive your message or intent – what you do at the beginning
▪ how you deliver the message, or do what you say you are going to do – the middle
▪ how you make sure people have received and understood what you have said or done – how you finish.

How well you manage these three things will determine the likelihood of your listener receiving your message clearly, and with the intended meaning. On that first date, my partner had inadvertently badly 'prepared' me to receive his level of interest and commitment, by asking an important personal question and then not paying proper attention to the answer (see, he is still paying today, poor guy).

When a client comes to me for coaching, I usually begin by listening for clues in how they structure their overall communication to me. The words that come out of our mouths, what we choose to reveal, and in what order, allow us to glean insights into guiding personal values, self-confidence, self-awareness and where the easy, 'low-hanging fruit' opportunities for improvement are.

Over the years, I have noticed that many people believe they have a good understanding of structure. Others recognise that they don't know what makes it good or bad. We are exposed to various kinds of structural approaches to face-to-face communication throughout our lives – at school or university, from our cultural influences, from the people around us and in our own accumulation of habits and experience. We are mostly aware of what has worked and what hasn't.

So what does this mean for you? Ask yourself these questions:

- Do you find that you have been told, or perhaps you feel, that you ramble, talk too much, take too long to get to the point or sound muddled? Do you hold back in social or work situations, afraid that you can't express your thoughts clearly? Or do you wonder why those you're talking to don't seem to have 'got' what you mean?
- Do you touch people while you speak, particularly early in conversations – either poke, lightly touch or put your body close to others while you engage in conversation?
- Do you find it hard to know where to 'start' a conversation, and take some time to get warmed up?
- Are you often surprised when you find out later that someone completely misinterpreted what you meant/said, or that they have had an emotional response you hadn't expected?

If you've answered yes to any or all of these, there may well be something wrong with the way you are structuring your messages.

Prepare

Aristotle said that 'the beginning is half of the whole', so let's begin at the beginning. Remember I said that 'prepare' means how you lay the ground for someone to receive your message or intent – what you do at the beginning of your communication. It is how you use your first few seconds or minutes, and how you manage your first impression.

How you prepare people to receive your message has a particular power. It is here that people form their most lasting impressions. It is the hardest place from which to recover, and regular abuse of it can create confusions that take years to clarify.

The most common type of mismanagement of 'prepare' comes when we intentionally or unintentionally create physical or verbal distractions. These, in effect, muddy the waters of our message/meaning before the listener has had time to take it in. This in turn makes the message harder to understand, and may create a wildly different meaning from the one you expected.

As we proceed, keep in mind that there is no one best way to get it right. The measure of how well we have done in a particular setting depends on whether we have communicated our intended meaning. Impressions, after all, are just that. They don't have to be right to matter.

 case study Hector: mismanaging first impressions

Hector is a young man with a lot of responsibility. He has a steady job, a young family and a bright future. He is part of the tribe of bright and successful people who have emerged in the last ten years and are now in fairly senior management positions, with the promise of running the shop before their first wrinkle appears.

Hector called me because he was having conflicts with people he worked with. He had begun to hear people describe him as a bit 'difficult' and 'hard to get to know'.

When we met and he spoke about this, I noticed something strange about how I was feeling. He was distracting me from his message very early on in our conversation, particularly when he spoke about a sensitive issue or gave an answer to a direct question. Despite the fact that he had called me in to deal with this very problem, he gave the impression that he didn't care about how he was affecting people. Here is how he did it.

As he began speaking, he firmly withheld eye contact. And I don't mean that he kept his eyes down or slightly to the side as shy or nervous people sometimes do. He literally didn't look at me for many seconds, and sometimes had his eyes almost closed, as if I was not in the room. (Try this in conversation with a friend and you'll see how uncomfortable it makes you both feel.) It confused me at the time because he was communicating a combination of don't care/not interested and painful shyness. Then, mid-thought, he resumed eye contact for an instant and disappeared again at the start of a new thought. He did this over and over again throughout our conversation. While he was speaking, he made eye contact at intervals, as if he was checking in with me, but was not interested enough to see if I was listening. This was particularly apparent when he talked about anything sensitive or personal.

Because of this lack of eye contact – or rather 'anti' eye contact – by the time we got into the meat of our discussion, I was reeling from the distractions and was really not able to listen properly. I could understand what others had been going through: all of this created an impression that he was defensive, aloof, arrogant and not interested.

As I questioned him, Hector volunteered the information that as a child he was told that he should be seen and not heard. His parents were strict disciplinarians, and he attended an equally strict boarding school. For most of his life he had felt that he should either approach people with his ideas almost by apologising first, or should say nothing. The lack of eye contact was not humility, he explained, but a habit that came from feeling embarrassment at expressing individuality or opinions.

I asked Hector to practise a difficult exercise that would deal with his discomfort as he 'prepared' people to receive his message. I asked him to make full eye contact with me for three seconds before he spoke, and again at the beginning of each new 'thought'. This may not sound like a long time, but for Hector it felt like an eternity.

At first, it proved very difficult for him and the process was a bit mechanical – as newly introduced behaviours often are. But after about a half an hour of practising and role-playing in a range of types of conversations he would have to go through in the future – face to face with his team, at a business cocktail party, at a round-table discussion, in a conversation with his kids' teachers at parents' evening – he began to become aware of and articulate the motivation behind the old behaviours. As if a light had gone on, he associated the behaviours with his beliefs about himself.

After this discussion, Hector started visibly to relax, and I felt more engaged and positive about him as he spoke. As he put it, we had 'brought the monster into the daylight'. Those three seconds were enough to let it out!

Hector has since reported to me that he has had fewer conflicts with colleagues, and has started to have what he calls 'better conversations earlier' with people he meets for the first time. He said his wife noticed positive changes almost immediately – even over Saturday breakfast surrounded by noisy kids, he seemed more interested in their conversations. The distractions Hector created were linked to his self-esteem and years of deflecting attention away from himself at a critical time in his communication – the beginning. He needed to get past his barrier of not believing his message was worthy of being heard and of drawing attention away from things that were important to him.

Now it is up to Hector to keep up the good work.

 case study Lydia:
the impression backfiring

Lydia is a well-educated activist, mother and businesswoman. The kind of super-person many of us know, who always looks good, shows up to parent–teacher meetings after a hard day's work, travels, cooks and reads. She has political aspirations and spends a lot of time meeting new people and rallying support in public forums. She also attends a lot of cocktail parties, dinners, and small group and one-to-one discussions. She seems to have it all – including some feedback from a mentor that she gets on people's nerves.

I was introduced to Lydia by her mentor and we had coffee together one afternoon to discuss this 'getting on people's nerves' feedback. I found that she was a good listener, articulate and funny. So what was she doing wrong?

I suspected that the problem would be best seen in context, so I offered to accompany her to her next few public sessions, to observe and listen.

At our first cocktail party, I saw it. Whenever Lydia was introduced to a new person and asked to explain her position on an issue, she turned into someone else. Someone I had not met at the coffee shop. She leant in slightly too far to shake hands – I could see the other person move back. At the same time, she spoke slightly too loudly – louder than the other person – and smiled slightly too broadly. It was very subtle. She would touch them on the upper arm or poke them playfully – sometimes once, sometimes twice. She also got a little close while doing it. Occasionally she would preen someone's clothes, removing a (fictitious?) piece of lint from a lapel. She moved like a butterfly through the groups, and looked completely at ease. She didn't realise that she was cutting a path of destruction.

When we met back in our cosy coffee shop two weeks and three cocktail parties later, I demonstrated to her what I had observed her doing over the past weeks, and explained what I had seen her conversation partners doing as a result – backing away, leaning away, looking uncomfortable, relieved to get away. Lydia had developed a behaviour she felt was working for her and was a way of ensuring she was engaging people. She got their attention all right, but not in the way she intended.

I asked Lydia to try some new behaviours that more closely matched her intention to build a rapport with people. I asked her to physically slow down her initial approach, walk up to people more slowly, relaxing her hands at her side until the time came to shake hands, rather than come up with her hand already high for shaking. Instead of starting with the first question and controlling the conversation, I asked her to smile, greet the person gently, and pause. By doing this, she was in effect creating a moment for something else to happen. It was frightening for her, this quiet space between meeting and speaking. It took a few practice runs, but eventually she got the hang of it. At the same time, I asked her to shift her weight more evenly on the soles of her feet instead of leaning forwards. This subtle shift helped her to breathe a little more naturally and slowly – making it easier to wait.

After a few sessions of simple body-weight shifts, pausing, and allowing the conversation to be directed more evenly between her and others, she found that she invited more natural responses from people. She began to discuss a broader range of topics with strangers. She said she laughed more with people. Her many conversations became a more like a dance than a roll call!

I think of the 'prepare' stage of face-to-face communication as necessitating a heightened state of awareness. What you do here can create obstacles that you have to work around, or it can make the rest of the conversation flow smoothly.

Deliver

Think of 'deliver' as the way you package and string your thoughts together, how you convey what you want to say. The key is to choose an appropriate structure or approach, based on both what you have to achieve and the sort of people you are talking to. You need to arrange your messages so that they come out the way you want them to, and are received the way you intended.

Most of us have been accused now and then of getting lost or off track while we are talking or telling a story. Some of us ramble, repeat ourselves, feel rushed by others to hurry up and finish, or perhaps notice a look of confusion or irritation on the face of the person we are talking to. Have you ever been interrupted or asked to get to the point?

It is not all your fault. Part of the challenge lies with your listener. The truth is, we all have a preferred way of receiving information. Some of us like it to be delivered straight and to the point, short and sweet, while others enjoy the detail and prefer to take the time to let the picture build up.

So the answer to 'how do I stop rambling?' or, 'how do I know which is the right structure?' is simply: it depends. Because every listener and context is different, the key is to choose well, based on what you know could be the best way for the listener to understand.

Let's start with the fact that the more you know about how your listener needs to hear something, the more likely this is to happen. How you put it all together depends on which category of structure type it falls into. There are two main categories of these, based on intention – Inform and Persuade – and they will get you through most of the situations you face.

Structure one: when your listener needs to be informed

What if someone you are talking to just wants to be educated or informed of something? They might for instance need the answer to a request such as, 'How do you bake that cake?' or, 'What was your favourite part of the holiday?' or, 'Please update me on the progress of the project' or, 'Tell me about the changes to the policy.'

There are two things you can do to increase the likelihood of your message being received and understood by others:

1 Before speaking, know the point you are trying to make. One mistake many people make is that when asked to inform, they don't consider what their point is before they launch into an answer. Ask yourself what you want your listener to do or think as a result of what you are about to say. Only when you know the answer to this question should you speak.

2 Then, only talk about the areas that support your point. The other mistake comes from the realm of the 'subject matter expert'. Often people who know a lot about a subject don't know where to start – or finish – simply because there is so much they *could* say. The result is too much information. Again, the focus is not on the listener but on the talker.

Structure two: when your listener needs to be persuaded

When you need to persuade or convince someone of something, it is your job to be relevant enough to change the way they think or act. Usually when you have to change someone's mind, it is your position or experience versus theirs, so knowing as much as you can about them is vital. In Chapter Six, I address listening styles in some detail. One of the biggest mistakes people make when trying to persuade is that they feel passionately about their position, so they argue it beautifully. The problem is they don't make the leap to the listener – they have not gathered any information on how their audience is going to make a decision, or on the factors that such a decision depends upon. I remember spending a couple of days working with a client who was crafting an employment package for a man he was trying to hire from a competitor. The salary was significantly better than the man was earning at the time, and the move to a new location included an apartment, driver and all expenses paid. There was a plan put together for his future career, his children to be in new top schools and his wife to join the top local golf club. After two weeks of deliberation, the candidate refused the offer. Despite weeks spent chasing this man, what they didn't know about him was that he was considering 'pro-tirement'. He wanted to spend more time tending to his garden and to be a more 'hands-on dad' with his young children from his second marriage. He wanted to work a couple of days a week from his home office, and the new employer wanted him to work full time from the city office. Had they known that this was what he wanted, would the offer have been any different? Perhaps. The employer worked very hard to come up with a package that was 'better' that the one he had, without considering, or asking, what he was looking for.

 case study **Robin: the smart guy who is incomprehensible**

I met Robin at a dinner party. I was sitting on the opposite side of the table, a few seats away, and I watched those around him one by one either get up and move somewhere else on the table, or turn away physically and make it impossible for him to join in a three-way conversation. I was far away enough to observe this –

the guy that no one wants to sit next to – but not close enough to hear what anyone was saying. I started to feel sorry for him, but curious at the same time. What was going on? Could it be that he had bad breath or was just boring? Did he speak some foreign language that no one knew? Well, sort of.

I made eye contact, smiled and got up to go and sit in the empty seat next to him. I soon learned that he was a technical specialist in the thermal properties of solids. Aside from, 'Hello, how do you like the party?' I had little idea of what he was talking about. He did most of the talking, and responded to my questions without volleying a question back to me. His answers to personal questions (non-work-related) quickly circled back to his work (unintelligible). I believe that in these situations there is very little to lose for either of you if you employ a little honesty and kind confrontation – you never know where it will take you. It might even be more interesting than any other conversation you have that night. So, on behalf of all those people who have sat next to a person who bored them and never said anything, and to those condemned to the club of the avoided – I went for it.

After several more minutes of confusion from me – and uninterrupted talk from him – I asked him if he would mind me talking to him about something personal. His eyes lit up – and once I had assured him it wasn't what he was thinking, I told him that I had been with him for twenty minutes and that I didn't feel he was in any way listening to me or interested in what I had to say. He seemed taken aback, but encouraged me to expand. I told him what I had observed, that he talked too much and too long without involving the person he was speaking with. He also had a habit of doing what I call 'starting from the middle' – something highly analytical people have a tendency to do – which is to speak for a while without a context or a clearly stated subject up front. So the listener has to work hard to sort the sentences. Instead of,

'Our host was a speaker at an art conference last week (context) and in her speech she mentioned that very piece of art on the wall (subject) there. Isn't it beautiful?' Robin would say, 'I see what she means by beautiful. The art in here is really something isn't it?' The listener is confused either into attention or inattention.

'Starting from the middle' is a very common mismanagement of delivery. When someone, like Robin, is also very absorbed in their work or personal interests, they tend not to consider that their listener needs to put what they are saying into a relevant context. If you are one of these party bores (sorry), one sure remedy is to ask about the other person and figure out a way to make what you do relevant to them.

Robin joined me later that evening over coffee and wanted to pursue the matter further. He asked for some things he could practise in the weeks ahead. Here are the pointers I gave him:

■ Try to speak without using any technical jargon. Instead, choose an analogy or another word to describe what you do. This is harder than it looks!
■ When answering questions, limit the initial response to a short, say ten-word, answer. This is good practice for long-winded people.
■ Where possible, state a point or conclusion first – then do the explanation.

Try this out with a friend, because you are not likely to be able to do it on your own at first. Sometimes, what you think is a short answer isn't.

case study Craig: the rambler

I met Craig through a friend who was thinking of setting up a hedge fund and involving Craig as a partner. Craig is a very intelligent man who is renowned for being a subject-matter expert. One thing worrying his friend was the extent to which Craig's tendency to ramble – to talk too much and too long without a point – might affect their ability to get the business up and running quickly. They had to impress a lot of high-powered people in a short period of time to secure the funding they needed in order to grow.

I spent an afternoon with Craig discussing his plans for the business. He was aware of his partner's concerns, so we addressed them directly. I privately tested where the problem was coming from by listening and asking a number of questions that gave him an easy way to give me a direct answer. These questions resulted in long-drawn-out explanations. Even telling him this frankly and demonstrating a shorter, more direct way of answering didn't work. 'My colleagues always tell me I talk too much,' was his reply. He had a sly smile on his face as if he enjoyed the feedback and had no intention of changing it. 'It's just me.'

I could see I needed to understand more about him before proceeding. Detour!

After a while, I asked him to tell me a little more about how he felt about the start-up of this new business with his potential partner. He opened up and explained that it was very scary for him. He felt frightened that he would be leaving the comfort of a salary with a big firm for the wilds of the jungle of small start-ups. He had an academic background and had been working for big companies all his life. He had written articles about his subject, been sought after for his advice, and was considered a guru in his chosen field. He was comfortable with this and was frightened of the risk associated with the move to his own small business.

At this point, I asked him again why he thought he had difficulty with short, direct answers and explanations. He paused, then eventually said that he didn't think a short answer had as much value as a long one. More material and more exploration meant value. As an aside, he said that he had always felt secretly guilty that he got paid too much for what he did, and if anyone found out how easy it all was he would be denounced as an impostor!

Now, where from here? I assured him that many others felt the same way and that we wouldn't solve that here – but suggested that we look at some of the behaviours that might be reinforcing that feeling and keeping him from moving past it. I promised him that, although he would be uncomfortable at first, with persistence he would see gradual changes over the next few weeks.

Aside from Craig's very long and rambling responses, there were a number of physical things going on at the same time:

■ His posture while seated was such that he 'crushed' his middle – his core. He either hunched over his paperwork on the table or sat very low in his chair, creating a very enclosed space in the centre of his body. His chest and belly were not open.
■ He often gestured with slow, circular motions.
■ When he did pause, it was not with eye contact. And it was usually for a breath.

Craig's discussion came across as if it was with himself. Convincing himself – not looking for understanding or acceptance from others. He lacked structure to his response, making it difficult to determine what he considered important or of particular priority. Like sheet music but with a fairly random selection of notes.

Trying to fix it all at once would be too much, so we addressed the non-physical side first. We started with a simple explanation of a common-sense way to approach structuring most of his responses, particularly in a business context. Like Robin, Craig was in the habit of 'diving into the middle' of his content. The listener had to derive their own context or wait for it to become clear. (It is too much to expect the listener to structure what you are saying for you – most won't.) We then addressed his posture. He wasn't aware of 'crushing' his middle and his chest, nor of his round gestures and lack of eye contact. We worked on these postural elements, and finally the circular gesturing disappeared.

I ran into Craig not long ago, having not seen him for six months. He looked very different. He had lost weight, seemed to be taller – I think it was his improved posture – had shaved off his beard, and had a new girlfriend! He told me he never had joined the hedge fund but instead left the finance business and joined his girlfriend in a small business, selling landscaping design and materials. You never know what standing up straight can bring.

Make sure

This is the part of your communication where you need to be sure people have understood what you have said. Paying attention at this stage is one of the most important and most difficult things to do. But the rewards of getting it right are powerful. By the time you reach this stage in a communication, you have done most of the work. Now for the final hurdle, a critical one. If you have been mismanaging your 'make sure', you may hear from others that you:

* sometimes assume too much
* don't acknowledge other people's contribution enough
* perhaps lose attention quickly or finish before others and move on to the next 'thing'

Other clues include: not checking to see if people understand or accept what you say or do before you finish; listening long enough only to start talking about yourself again; not finishing your sentences, or finishing other people's sentences for them.

 case study John: too little too late

John is a successful banker, 32 years old and on his second marriage. He plays polo and raises ponies, and with whatever spare time he has he flies for long weekends to Africa on a private jet. He runs a major trading desk in London, and is a powerful business developer. He is known to start strong, hunt the deal, get it done and move on. I came in contact with him because he was fearful of losing a major deal he had been chasing. He was sure the client was going to give him the business because 'all the signals were there' – they had a great relationship. Then he received an emergency call, all could be lost. Help!

You may well ask how anyone could have got so far in business without having a heightened sense of awareness of what was going on around him. The key lies in John's behaviour towards others. He often interrupts – not rudely, but he completes other people's sentences enthusiastically and with great charm. In the time I was observing him, I never saw him check other people's understanding or address concerns directly. This created the impression amongst clients (those I asked) that they could not confide in him, or ask him a 'dumb' question. He came across as impatient, important and terribly busy. He was indeed impatient and terribly busy, but nobody is so important that they can afford to ignore this impression.

As I spoke with him, the cause of the problem became clear. He had assumed he understood what was going on with the client at many critical moments in the lead up to his present situation. He had moved on these assumptions, taken action, and then discovered that he had very little understanding of the client's motivations and very little reading of what was actually going on. At the eleventh hour, he found out that the client felt he didn't understand the most important issues around the reasons why he was making the decision. John was focusing more on what he 'did' – the tasks and the order of those things – than checking to see if they were the right things to be doing.

Interestingly, as I talked to John, I observed that his body was also 'moving on', starting to turn or lean away as he appeared to feel nearer his conclusions. He would finish a thought mid-sentence and move on to another. It was as if his body was figuratively walking out of the room. His eye contact became less and less as he felt he had made his point. This was reinforcing the impression that he had already figured it out and nothing more needed to be discussed.

When I told him about my observation, he became visibly angry and frustrated. It was clear that the only way he was going to fix it was to do something he felt very uncomfortable with.

He had to go back to the client face to face and 'make sure' – to check his assumptions and ensure that what he was doing was understood and accepted. He needed to acknowledge that he had missed some important signals and would ask the client how to fix the situation. By now, though, deadlines were imminent, and the likelihood of repairing the damage was slim. John was so far away from where he needed to be that the gap was too big to fill. Significantly, he revealed a similar chain of events in the breakdown of his first marriage: by the time he realised what was wrong, the gulf was too wide and it was too late to fix it.

He ended up losing the business. The clients didn't want a follow-up meeting or to discuss it any more. It wasn't that they were angry, but they described it as being like a relationship where 'we got used to each other and stopped listening'. The team who won the business was more 'interested' and 'made efforts to help them think about their own business in a different way'.

There were opportunities for gathering insight that had passed John by. By making assumptions and not paying attention, he had trodden on any trust he had built up. When he had the solution, he couldn't make the calls, he couldn't own the problem. He wanted to ignore it in the hope that it would sort itself out or go away. He also didn't finish with me – didn't call me back or keep me involved. It wasn't until several weeks later that I got a call asking to talk. (Too late again?)

John's bad habits were reinforced by a career of being rewarded for fast-moving big starts. Things had changed as the stakes got higher. After we had met for the first time, he started to think about the subject, and noticed that wife number two was beginning to complain of the same things we were talking about in the client context: he was a big-game hunter – lots of attention upfront for the chase, and then off to the next challenge.

He was keen to fix the problem but also knew it would take some doing.

We started with little things. I asked John to do some simple things no one would notice except him. A very good place to start was by practising acknowledgement. I set him the task of finding some things he could acknowledge every day – from something someone did well at work, his children, his partner, random encounters with strangers. I suggested he contact someone he forgot to acknowledge for a kindness, sent a thank-you note, or marked a forgotten birthday. I explained that it could also involve a private acknowledgement of being grateful for simple things like his health and his beautiful family. It would take seconds, he could do it quietly to himself, and I asked for him to do a minimum of seven a day. At the beginning, I asked him to focus on acknowledging completed things, even things he had done himself.

Also, to help him improve his personal and client relationships, I asked him to set up face-to-face meetings where the primary objective was to do a reality check, to confirm that there was no mismatch of understanding or commitment in their dealings so far. To ensure he was probing thoughts and feelings, the conversation had to include follow-up questions such as, 'Tell me more about that' and, 'Why do you feel that way?' and paraphrasing what the other person had said – 'So as I understand it, you would like to see...is that right?' or, 'Have I addressed your concerns?'

I asked him to be aware of how he shifted his weight while he was speaking to others. People like John often create the feeling through their body that they have finished. John had some very easily identifiable movements. He would subtly sit or stand facing away almost from the beginning of the conversation, then as it got nearer to his finish he drifted away, weight slightly on his heels if he was standing, body turned further away if he was sitting, ready to make his escape (almost as if he was never going to commit to being there to begin with).

I asked John at first only to practise putting his weight equally on both feet – more awareness on the front of the feet – at the beginning of new conversations, and to have his shoulders and pelvis aligned facing the person he was speaking to, hands resting however he felt comfortable. This may sound simple, but it was uncomfortable for John. The desire to shift his body away and his weight back on his heels was enormous. I told him he could anchor himself if he needed to by gently putting a hand to rest, or leaning ever so slightly on a chair back or table top if there was one around. Staying forward and aligned was key.

He commented that he found it difficult to think about what he was saying while he was practising this new alignment. This is a normal response when you add new behaviours. It is like when someone points out to you that you are holding your tennis racquet in the wrong way, and when you correct it you start to miss the ball!

Here are some things John said he did that helped him most:

» He decided to schedule one or two extra face-to-face meetings with clients, with the primary objective of reaffirming mutual commitment to bring the project or deal to completion.

» If he was working with a team, he would acknowledge everyone's contribution individually, and express his appreciation to people for their assistance. (His secretary was so surprised, she blushed.)

» He made a company-wide announcement thanking the team for their contribution.

» He cleaned his closet and a very messy top drawer (yes, that's what he said!)

When you want to be understood more often, you need to start by understanding your listener better, so that what you are saying to them makes sense and is relevant to them. Combine that with common-sense principles, such as first knowing your point and then saying only what you need to say to support the point. People listen best when you have prepared them to receive your message, delivered what you said you would, and then done what you could to be sure they have understood it in the way you intended. Some of the world's best ideas end up in the rubbish bin. That doesn't have to happen to yours.

chapter four

confrontation is an invitation

One thing that has troubled me greatly over the years is seeing wonderful people trapped in situations they are not happy with, because the prospect of confrontation seems more painful than the situations themselves. I have also come across intelligent, talented people whose fear of what 'someone might say', or of the possibility of a reaction they can't handle, has kept them from doing something they would really like to do.

Be comforted with the knowledge that, if handled sensitively, confrontation can be both a positive and a rewarding experience.

In this chapter, I will deal with a common thread that runs through most of the difficult situations I coach, which is that somewhere lurking at the heart of most problems is how we deal with confrontation – how well we either give it or receive it, the act of confronting or being confronted. I will consider both because being able to cope well with one will make you better at coping with the other.

Few of us are perfectly comfortable telling others what we think when we think it needs to be said, and most of us are reluctant to speak up. It is a lot easier to talk to someone else about how awful it is when another person doesn't express how they really feel or how they hurt your feelings, did a bad job or drove you crazy, than it is to actually look into the eyes of the person concerned and tell them.

Do any of the following sound like you?

■ 'I don't like confrontation because usually it has not gone well in the past.'
■ 'I am concerned that if I confront the problem I might just escalate it.'

- 'I might be rejected, or destroy the friendship.'
- 'I might get surprises I am not ready for.'
- 'They might fight back.'
- 'Maybe I don't want to know the truth.'
- 'They might get emotional.'
- 'I might get emotional.'
- 'I might hurt their feelings.'
- 'Maybe it's something I did and I am part of the problem.'

Are you one of those who think you know how the confrontation situation will end up: you play it through in your mind and imagine every problem and even the other person's response – 'I know how she will react' – until you get so uptight about what you need to say that you are too stressed to keep a clear head? If so, you are wasting your time. The chances are that you don't know how it is going to end. If you use some of the techniques in this chapter, you will be in a better position to orchestrate the ending.

Let me give you some important principles to keep in mind in case you are ever in doubt in a confrontational situation:

- Don't take it personally. Whatever the other person thinks or feels, it is not your problem. It is their problem, because it is their way of looking at the world. They see the world through their eyes. It is up to you to decide whether you want to get involved in someone else's problems.
- You are entitled to your own opinions and feelings, and to express them to yourself and others.
- You are entitled to ask for what you want, although you should realise that the other person is entitled to refuse you.
- You are entitled to change your mind.
- You are entitled to privacy.

- You are entitled to achieve your goals and aspirations as long as you do not take unfair advantage of someone else.
- Sometimes the decisions you make will be the wrong ones. So what? Accept the mistakes, don't take them too personally and try again.

I know this is not easy. Also, you shouldn't expect to do it right every time. None of us does. The reasons behind why we are or are not comfortable can be complex and troublesome.

Most people associate confrontation with something negative. It is that situation you have been dreading – there may be a lot at stake or you risk being embarrassed or humiliated. It is the thing you have mastered the art of avoiding. It may be the reason you never stick your neck out. I have found that the desire to avoid confrontation is the greatest single cause of inertia for people's careers. It is also statistically proven to be the underlying reason for most marriages and business partnerships breaking down. I have seen many clever business people get wiped off the career radar because they don't handle confrontation well – everything from being unable to ask for a pay rise to not performing in a difficult situation.

The key to confronting or to being confronted well lies in having the right attitude. After all, confrontation does not interfere with life, it is a precondition of life. Embracing rather than avoiding it is a healthy approach.

It's interesting to note that the word confrontation starts with con, which (from its Latin origin) means 'with' – together with someone. Not against. My grandmother used to say to me that 'opportunity is missed by most people because it is dressed in overalls and looks like work'. Well, she was right. With a different perspective, you can stop avoiding confrontation and instead start using it to your advantage.

Before you tell yourself, 'Yeah, easy to say but I now have to go out and do it' – suspend your disbelief. I would like you to see confrontation as an opportunity. An opportunity to help your career, strengthen and deepen your relationships and even help others around you. You don't have to choose between being honest and being effective – there is nothing to stop you being both. In your relationships, if you and your partner can find a way of talking about the things that are most important to you (particularly emotional issues) in a neutral and respectful way, you stand a better chance of staying together.

Confrontation styles

We all have a natural confrontation style we adopt most of the time, whether on the giving or receiving end. Understanding your own style and the style of the person you are dealing with will add a powerful element of control and confidence. Knowing a bit more about confrontation styles will increase your self-awareness and your awareness of others.

As I promised at the start of this book, we will not be delving into the psychological origins of your personal style. Rather we will look at what we can observe, and work from there.

I like to refer to four main confrontation styles that I call Aggressive, Controlling, Submissive and Active, and they are linked to the behavioural types I discussed in Chapter Two. I will also add another, Aspirational. Most of us aren't there, but as with anything aspirational, we can pluck from it when we need to.

Aggressive
This is the style generally associated with the Command and Control type. An Aggressive type is comfortable with

confrontation and sees it as almost an essential part of communication – on both the giving and receiving end. There are varying degrees of Aggressive, but generally the same characteristics are present.

Because Aggressives value an efficient use of time and generally prefer others to be direct and to the point, they can come across as abrupt and may interrupt you or finish your sentences for you. In their mind, confrontation equals efficiency.

They are often straightforward, speak in conclusions and commands, even accusations. They tend to make people around them feel inhibited, demoralised or at best exhausted at having to 'battle' with them. They are often accused of looking after their own needs over others'.

Physically, Aggressives' bodies are erect and they often stand still while talking, with very little upper body movement. They often clench their fists, or have their arms folded in front of them. They may shout, point or slam the table or door. Their breathing is often high in their chest, creating tension and rigidity in the shoulder and neck area. (I know this sounds too sweeping to be true, but believe me – I have seen these patterns repeating themselves over and over again.)

 ### *case study* Oscar: dealing with aggression swiftly

Most people would consider Oscar to be what is popularly known as an alpha male: successful, determined, life in order. He does most of the talking and controls the subject of his conversations, which are short, focused and usually end with something for the other person to do. He sets the agenda.

I had been working with members of Oscar's team, but hadn't come into contact with the man himself until I was called to see him a few days later. He proceeded to yell at me about something that had happened to one of his team members in the course of my work with them. His voice was really loud and he had decided to bawl me out in front of everyone, just outside his office. I was amazed. My first instinct was to smile because I couldn't believe it was happening. Wrong! This made it worse and the whole thing spiralled downhill over the next few minutes. When he had finished, I asked quietly if we could continue in his office, but he told me that he had said all he had to say and sent me on my way.

I was flabbergasted and spent some of the rest of the day phoning his associates to clarify the problem. Their response was, 'You aren't on the map until Oscar has yelled at you.' Was that supposed to be good?

By the end of the day I understood what had happened to upset him. Apparently, one of his team members had been embarrassed by one of the role-plays and ended up in tears because she felt humiliated in front of her colleagues. Despite having been on the receiving end of his response, I give Oscar credit here – he was upset because of his loyalty to his staff.

I knew I needed to address the problem quickly, so I called Oscar's assistant later the same week to arrange an appointment. In our meeting, I explained that I now understood his concern, listened to his point of view (which he expressed in a normal voice), corrected where necessary and finished by restating what we had agreed to in the first place. It ended peacefully and I continued to work with his team.

One of the drawbacks of this style is that Aggressives tend not to react well to being confronted. They are fine at dishing it out, but I have yet to meet one who can take it with the same flair. They are not flustered by a direct, like-with-like approach, but be aware that if it goes wrong and they feel cornered, they will attack – verbally, intellectually, hopefully not physically. It is like the old adage that if you show fear, an angry dog will attack. Sometimes, though, an angry dog will attack an angry dog!

However, you can improve your chances of getting through:

How to confront an Aggressive style
- Make an appointment to see the person – don't just show up and confront them.
- Be sure to do your homework.
- Don't apologise, agree, or make excuses.
- Be direct and well structured – tell them you disagree but ask them to explain their views further.
- Don't let them interrupt you.
- Avoid sounding upset or angry.
- Conclude by restating what you have resolved/agreed.
- Maintain eye contact; keep your body upright and relaxed.

Controlling

This style is consistent with the Rationalise, Employ Logic and Order person of Chapter Two. Controllers have an analytical mind that is more interested in the task and the process than in the people involved. They can be elegant arguers because of their grasp of the facts and memory recall, but exasperating for those who seek quick solutions or who rely on intuition. Under pressure, Controllers can easily slip into being verbal bullies, but they rarely exaggerate and name-call, so bullying will feel more like stubbornness.

Physically, they are fairly low-key. When confronting or being confronted they are not emotional and their faces show little expression. This doesn't mean they don't feel it, they just don't/can't show it. I have seen Controllers in confrontational situations who, instead of demonstrating empathetic responses, show inappropriate physical reactions, as if trapped emotional energy needed to get out and found a 'leak' somewhere in their body. This can be quite distracting! A loud sigh at an odd time, a sarcastic remark, a jerky shift in their chair, a tilting of the head (usually back), staring for a long period at some place on the floor as if processing something, wringing of the hands, are all typical of these physical tics.

 ### *case study* Alan: balancing thoroughness with action

I met Alan when we were sitting on the same board for a smart, dynamic, charity advisory group. I soon discovered that his skills as a lawyer were an obvious benefit to the group, but that his confrontation style was going to present a challenge. Alan was an expert in his field, experienced and well respected. He was also a classic Controller. The group, however, was full of young, dynamic people out to create something different in the charity world. Alan believed that he was there to save them from themselves, to keep them from imploding and to guide them through the hazards they may face. This was certainly the right intention – but his inability to tailor his style to suit the group turned out to be a minefield.

During the meetings, the team would present ideas and project plans to the board that they wanted to implement. In the beginning, it was a struggle because Alan would find a detail missing in a spreadsheet or a minor issue that needed double-checking, and would hold the whole project up until it was corrected. But he didn't confront these issues in the meeting where the board could have agreed or disagreed, or even solved the problem on the spot. Instead, he would take the information away, study it and get back to them in a week with a list of minutiae he wanted confirmed.

This was bogging down the team's progress and dampening their enthusiasm. What was Alan going to find next?

I was asked to confront him about it (there's a surprise!). It is always best not to confront this type with an audience present, so I asked Alan to join me for lunch where I could bring the issue up over dessert.

I was able to make him aware that, much as the young, dynamic group valued his advice, they also had to be able to act on it – they had deadlines to meet and we needed to find a way to balance thoroughness with action. We agreed to send him as much detail as possible before the meeting so that he could present his findings on the day. And we appointed someone from the charity to liaise with him directly on any potential legal issues as they happened, so that they were less likely to become an issue in the meetings.

To confront Alan the Controller successfully, I needed to be confident I wasn't going to embarrass him and to ensure he was part of the solution.

How to confront a Controlling style

■ Make sure you do your homework – they will know the detail.
■ State what you see as the problem – don't offer a solution yet. Alternatively, let them start: ask them for a detailed explanation of what they believe the issue/problem is, and listen to their answer.
■ Paraphrase back to them.
■ If you disagree, say so and explain why.
■ Avoid judgements and have your facts and examples ready.
■ Tell them that you would like to be able to come to them again should the problem continue.

Submissive

The Submissive style is generally associated with the Get
Friendly, Seek Harmony type I outlined in Chapter Two. These
types tend to sacrifice their own needs in favour of others' and
may be put upon or unfairly taken advantage of. They know
they should say something, but don't – either because of a bad
experience in the past or out of habit.

The really positive thing about Submissive people is that
they are usually loyal supporters and skilled empathisers. But
equally, they can end up irritating others because they may be
perceived as people who don't stand up for themselves – so
why should others stand up for them?

Physically, people of this type may keep a low profile, by
slightly rounding their shoulders, clasping their hands below
their waist (in front or behind), making little eye contact,
speaking softly and prefacing anything they say with, 'I wonder
if you wouldn't mind' or, 'I'm terribly sorry to bother you
but...'or, 'I'm sorry, I'm really sorry, but...' In this way, they
present themselves to others in a manner that sounds unsure
or lacking in confidence.

Even worse, they may stay silent when they wish they
had said something – all the noise is happening on the inside.
If it is held in long enough it may find that it channels out
in unhealthy ways, like inappropriate anger at the wrong
person or thing, resentment, addictions, depression and other
physical illnesses.

Usually this style is uncomfortable both with confronting and
with being confronted.

case study Kate: safety in numbers

Kate is a very intelligent and capable woman who runs her own boarding kennels. She is a very generous and loving person with the dogs – she just has a problem with people. She has a typical Submissive confrontation style. She used to let her clients get away with leaving dogs longer than promised, forgetting to pick them up, bringing dogs over without an appointment and bringing in sick dogs for her to take care of.

The problem emerged because her staff had to start picking up the excess work and were getting tired and stressed, doing weekends and late nights.

Kate's assistant called me to say that her team was meeting on a Saturday morning to talk about how they should approach her. The key was to find a solution that everyone could work with, then communicate it to Kate without hurting her feelings. They asked me to come along.

As a result of our meeting, we came up with some recommendations we could make to Kate, informally, to see what she thought.

We then organised a coffee-and-cake meeting the following Saturday with Kate, under the guise of a 'team idea factory'. Here are the outcomes.

To get started, we suggested the creation of some formal 'policies' around business opening and closing hours, drop-off and pick-up times and minimum expectations from owners. We proposed that it should be communicated face to face with each owner, one by one, and accompanied by a one-page checklist. The owners would sign a letter of understanding following the conversation and leave with a gentle but clear awareness of the new consequences in place for abuse of the rules.

We created a clearly stated goal that made the changes objective rather than personal:

'We have decided to put some policies in place to improve the management of the business and the overall care and safety of the dogs.'

We all then role-played some of the most common scenarios in which clients tried to 'break the rules':

'John, we agreed to the rules. Please don't ask me to break them.'

'We have a strict policy on adhering to pick-up times. If you need to leave her another day, just let us know twenty-four hours in advance.'

'Joe, your dog has an infection and we have a strict policy on not accepting sick dogs because of the risk to other dogs.'

Kate and the team were shown how to confront a problem by de-personalising it. This is crucial for easing the pain of confrontation, particularly with Submissive types. It can be confronting but at the same time non-threatening.

 case study Joanna: getting more amazing by being less amazing

Last year I sat next to a really lovely woman called Joanna on a long plane ride. She was troubled by her relationship with her mother-in-law, who really intimidated her, particularly at family gatherings. The more intimidated Joanna felt, the worse it seemed to get.

I asked Joanna to describe what it looked like – what was she doing when she felt intimidated and how things were getting, as she called it, 'worse and worse'. It emerged that her response to her feelings of intimidation was to do what I like to call 'get even more amazing'.

'Getting even more amazing' is the tendency to compensate by becoming nicer, more agreeable, more accommodating, more clever. Joanna's mother-in-law would quietly disapprove of many little things Joanna did during a dinner or gathering. Joanna would over-respond. Bigger gestures, bigger smiles, bigger apologies, bigger niceness. All the while she was seething inside.

This is a common response among Submissive confrontation types. The irony is that what they do in an attempt to make things better is often the very opposite of what they need to be doing.

I asked her to try a couple of things that would be the least obvious and give her the biggest benefit. The idea of confronting the mother-in-law directly about this habit might have been too much for Joanna to swallow. Rather, she was better off dealing with it on a case-by-case basis.

People in Joanna's situation have two powerful options: ignore it or call it. Both are a kind of tactical confrontation. Both happen the moment a jibe occurs. And regardless of which option she goes for, Joanna needs to remember that her mother-in-law's disapproval behaviours thrive on her (Joanna's) pain. She needs to understand that the jibes are not really about her – they are the mother-in-law's problem. To take them personally, to take responsibility for them, turns them into Joanna's problem and makes the situation worse.

Ignoring the jibes meant she (Joanna) wouldn't give them the oxygen they needed to survive, but that is always easier said than done. (I'll talk more about this later in the chapter.)

The second option is to call it. To acknowledge it and seek to understand it. Joanna's mother-in-law often delivered her jibes and disapprovals quietly to her so no one else could hear. It was important for Joanna to respond in the same way: quietly and directly.

Joanna and I practised some new responses, ordered another glass of wine and kept practising until we were in a fit of giggles.

The mother-in-law's most common disapprovals were stated as:

- 'I don't think that is appropriate.'
- 'We don't do it like that in our family.'
- 'You clearly don't know how to do it properly.'

Now Joanna was able to ask (with full eye contact and a calm and genuinely interested tone):

- 'Why do you feel that way?'
- 'What would you prefer?'
- 'Where did you get that information?'

Joanna and I swapped numbers, in part because I thought keeping tabs on her would spur Joanna into being brave enough to try out our rehearsed phrases, but also so that I could see how well my advice had or hadn't worked. Well, she called me a few weeks later after a regular family Sunday brunch, having tried a couple of her new responses. Her mother-in-law had been taken unawares and, having no clear reason for what she was saying, had retracted or backed down. Victory. Peace. At least until something else came up.

Also, dear Submissives, beware of using too much padding: you may take too long to get to your point, mention too many other things or 'sugar' the conversation so it becomes hard to recover and get back on track – the gap is too wide between your point and the time it took you to get there. You have made it too soft in order to lessen the impact on you and the other person, so you end up too far away from where you need to be.

How to confront a Submissive style
- Choose a neutral place to have the discussion – take a walk, go out of the office to a coffee shop, pick a comfortable space

- Don't put the other person under pressure – keep it informal
- Be careful to use facts and real examples – avoid judgements as you describe the issue/problem
- Say how the problem makes you feel
- Recommend a solution, or ask for their idea of a solution
- Be prepared to be part of the solution – offer to help if needed

Active

The Active style is most closely associated with the Feel it and Say it person mentioned in Chapter Two. Because of their comfort with self-expression, they tend to be disguised as the most at ease with confrontation. But this style has a chink in its expressive armour. Active types can confront, but tend to take being confronted as a blow to the ego. They can easily become judgemental of others. Of all the styles, they are the most willing to confront, but do not always do it in the most elegant manner. They can be aggressive, but this is tempered with a people-orientation. They usually have a high level of energy and enthusiasm that can be positive and motivating, but if not organised or controlled can misfire in confrontational situations.

In my experience, they are more often than not articulate under pressure; when others' tempers may be flaring, they can be cool and clear. (Equally, they could be the drama queens sulking in the corner. One drawback of this confrontation style is its unpredictability – they are the artistes of the confrontational world.) Physically, they move easily, gesture animatedly and are usually good storytellers.

Over the years I have been involved with many teams who take great care to select certain people within the team to answer the tough questions – to handle objections and misunderstandings. In one contract I had with a major international project, I was involved in coaching the team on one of the most important parts of the process – handling difficult and controversial (and sometimes personal) questioning from many different committees, under intense pressure. They had to do this skilfully, while continuing to build on their relationships with different influencers. It was the people with the Active style who most often excelled.

One key member of the team, a high-profile politician, seemed to be hooked on the need for high stakes surprise. This meant he would not rehearse the responses for the interrogations, but preferred to make it up on the spur of the moment. This made us all nervous (and me a bit angry). Because of his position, we couldn't replace him with someone more reliable or with a better team player. He was critical to the team's message and our ability to win.

To his credit, he pulled it off with only a few cringe-making blunders. I think in the end we all shamed him into getting it right, appealing to his ego – which was consistent with his Active confrontational style.

 case study Chloe: telling it like it is

Chloe is an entrepreneur I met while working with a long-standing client. She is one of those bright young things – grew her business on her own, edgy ideas, the beneficiary of an 'incubator' my clients set up to nurture talent and fund potentially worthwhile commercial ventures.

I remember the day we met: she was sitting on the floor of her office, surrounded by papers and clutter, and the first thing she said to me was, 'Hi – are you are the person Bill sent to keep me from putting my foot in my mouth?' The only thing I could say was 'Yes!'

It was time for Chloe to hit the road talking to banks and other financial institutions, to raise funding for her business. Chloe's problem was that she was described as 'a wild card' or 'unpredictable' and would say things that would make others feel as if she was being deliberately (and unnecessarily) provocative or unprepared. Both of these were true. Chloe had a particular characteristic of the Active confrontation style: 'ready–fire–aim'. She went for it – whatever it was – without thinking things through first. This might have been okay had there not been so much at stake. She was now spending other people's money and entering a world where everything she said in public could be noted and could affect her chances of success. She needed to switch to 'ready–aim–fire'.

As we discussed her situation, Chloe revealed that she had always felt that her 'tell it like it is' style had got her where she was today and that not saying what she was thinking was somehow not honest. But there is a difference between saying what you are thinking and honesty. I explained to her that while her instinct might be true, in order to make a transition to this next phase of her career she needed to change. Her directness would still be an asset – she just needed to control and focus it. Her investors needed to feel she could be relied upon to do what she said she would do, and these should be the right things.

Active confronters like Chloe need to prepare particularly well, so they don't fall back into their old way of responding. For example, before, Chloe would appear confident and speak with authority on her subject. But when she was asked a tough question, or if she thought that a listener was going down a path she didn't appreciate, she would take the bait and say something that embarrassed the other person or damaged her credibility: she would point out that a fact was wrong or make up an answer to something when 'I don't know' would have been sufficient.

We prepared her for these tough situations, rehearsed her on the kinds of things her listeners might ask or press her about. We removed the temptation to revert to her default reaction by giving her another option – the well-prepared response. Chloe took to preparation very well and didn't see it as removing any 'honesty' in her communication, but rather as helping her to help her listener – giving them what they needed to feel confident she could do the job. Chloe has since built and sold the business we worked on together. Latest reports are she is on her third!

How to confront an Active style
- Acknowledge the positive aspects of their contribution.
- Paint the big picture – make sure they understand the importance of what they are doing and how they fit into the wider concept and objective.
- Be direct, positive, use facts and examples.
- Avoid being judgemental, instead use terms such as, 'it's my impression' or, 'the impression that behaviour could create.'
- Ask them how they would like to solve the problem or make a recommendation.

Aspirational

The Aspirational person represents bits and pieces from all of us. There are not too many people I know (and I include myself when I say this) who manage to confront well, comfortably or consistently. However, where would we be if we didn't aspire to improve or to do something better? You may recognise in yourself the characteristics outlined below when you have confronted successfully. Keep chipping away at the characteristics you have that don't serve you and replace them with the characteristics of this style. All confrontation styles can usefully adopt aspirational characteristics.

When you confront well, it is because you have been concerned with respecting others and have been willing to negotiate and compromise where necessary. You keep your promises, are prepared to take risks and if you try something that doesn't work out, you don't take it too personally. You avoid negativity, focus on the positive, can motivate others and help them feel more positive about themselves.

You give genuine compliments and are prepared to receive them. You give an honest opinion and listen to other points of view. You endeavour to become a better communicator and more aware of the impact you have on others.

Some Aspirational style language includes:

- 'Tell me what you think about…'
- 'I feel…'
- 'What is your opinion…?'
- 'Let's…'
- 'How do you think we should deal with…?'

Physically, you are aware of listening with full attention to another point of view; your weight is usually balanced on both feet, your body is relaxed and you maintain eye contact while listening or speaking. Your jaw is relaxed, fingers relaxed, toes and feet relaxed.

You make an effort to create the right environment for open, honest communication. You have removed distractions, created some privacy, got comfortable, focused your attention.

case study Hiro: my hero

One of the best Aspirational style confronters I ever met was a client named Hiro, who had enormous responsibility in his job. He travelled the world regularly for work, managed businesses and people across time zones, had four lovely children, a supportive wife and a busy social and community life. And because he was so busy, he didn't have time for sloppy confrontation. He was caring, considerate, patient, and at the same time clear, objective, driven and effective. Everyone had nice things to say about him and he was admired by his peers and respected by his colleagues.

Sitting next to Hiro on (yet another) plane journey, I asked him for his thoughts on the secret to success. He explained to me quite simply that success revolved around knowing that you didn't know it all; the most successful people in life had smarter people around them. What he said reminded me of a famous epitaph: 'Here lies a man who had the courage to surround himself with people greater than himself.' Hiro guided his life according to this notion. He felt that he only succeeded when others around him succeeded. His humility was the key to his clarity and charisma.

This belief was reflected in everything he did and said. Hiro is certainly still an inspiration to me and, to this day, now retired from his busy job, he continues to be sought after as a problem-solver and mentor.

It may sound obvious to say that confronting and being confronted are two very different things, but the important point to understand here is that although they are similar, they require different approaches.

The secret to being more comfortable with confronting people is having a reliable structure you can use, so that you know what you have to say and in what order. With a structure you can feel more confident and in control.

On the other side, the secret to being more comfortable when you are confronted is to head for the context. Understanding what the person is really talking about or where they are coming from means you can deal with what has been handed to you appropriately – and with more confidence and control.

Confronting: the structure

You can confront anything if you understand there is a structure to it. Use the structure as your anchor, and hang on tight in heavy weather.   So how can structure help you confront with confidence? I promised you in Chapter Three that structure was about understanding how people best receive information, and how information is therefore best presented in a certain order depending on the person and the circumstance. The order and structure of your message can and will affect the way the other person hears your information and responds to you. You are more likely to get a positive outcome if you have been sensitive to this. You can rely on structure to help you muster the courage to give it a try – if only because it will markedly increase your chances of success. Think of it as your lucky charm!

Here is a small selection of proven, everyday structures that work. I have used them for years with my clients. No matter how awful confronting may seem to you, it is a bit like dancing. You never wanted to get out on the dance floor – until you did and now there's no stopping you! (Everyone looks silly, and that's half the fun.) It's the same with confronting. Stop taking it so seriously and try it.

Tackle some of the little things first – you know what they are. Send back the insipid soup at the restaurant, tell your flatmate to stop using household items without replacing them, ask for the extra blanket on the plane or the pillow at the hotel.

Structure 1: confronting someone you need

You have some tough news to deliver to someone at work or in a professional setting – possibly your housekeeper, babysitter or caregiver.

▪ Frame the problem as if you 'own' it yourself.

▪ Don't then state the problem. Instead, succinctly state the solution or action you want.

▪ Next, transfer the ownership of the problem.

▪ Make sure you repeat it and use the same language. It is common for the other person to introduce other issues or argue. Don't get sidetracked or involved with anything else, and don't justify your position.

▪ Listen for cooperation and play it back to them.

This is how this structure might work in practice:

1 'George, you are always coming in late' is accusatory and runs the risk of putting the other person on the defensive. Instead start with words like 'I'm concerned that...' or, 'I'd like to talk to you about something that is bothering me' or, 'I have a problem that needs addressing.'

2 'I need you to be here at nine o'clock every morning.' Personalise it. Make it 'I' not 'we'.

3 'How can you help me?' 'How will you solve this?'

4 'So you will catch the earlier bus from now on or get a ride with your partner so you can be here by nine o'clock.'

5 'So what you are saying is you can be here by nine o'clock every morning' or, 'Let me summarise what you have said.'

If you still get resistance, hang on in there. Don't let emotion creep in. Ask: 'What is blocking you from doing/achieving this?' Once you identify the blocker, stay objective and stick to how they may be able to find a solution.

Structure 2: confronting someone you care about

This one is good for spouses, teenagers, friends, family – for times when emotion gets in the way more easily, and there may be a history of approaching each other or arguing in a particular way. This may help you step out of the pattern.

- State the issue in one sentence.
- Give an example of the behaviour you want to change.
- Describe how you feel about it.
- Tell them what you think is at stake if the behaviour doesn't change.
- State how you may be contributing to the problem.
- State your desire to resolve the issue.
- Ask them to respond.

This is how this structure might work in practice:

1 'John, I really want to talk to you about the effect your behaviour is having on some of our friends.'

2 'I found out that at our party last weekend you drank too much and were rude to Karen about how you think she is a pushy parent.'

3 'I am embarrassed, and concerned about the consequences.'

4 'If you can't control your drinking at our parties I am worried that our friendships could be at stake.'

5 'I feel partly responsible because I could have stopped filling your glass so often or had a word with you earlier.'

6 'This is what I would like to resolve, John. You're drinking too much and this aggressive behaviour is the result.'

7 'I want to understand your perspective and what you think is going on. Please talk to me.'

Structure 3: business is business

This is all about returning something, complaining about bad service, a general 'I should have said something at the time' syndrome. Bear in mind that complaining when something is wrong is perfectly okay, indeed expected. Also, behave like a civilised person or you get what you deserve. Customers have rights, but be fair. No one wants to help a mean person. Nine times out of ten the person you are complaining to is not the source of the problem.

▪ Be sure to find the right person to complain to.
▪ State up front what you want the outcome to be, nicely, confidently and with full eye contact.
▪ If you don't get satisfaction immediately, keep your cool. Persist, this is where most people break down or give up.

This is how to apply this structure in practice:

1 Complaining to the wrong person is pointless. The further you are away from the source of the problem or from the person who is empowered to fix it, the more exhausting and frustrating it can be. I have a mantra that goes: 'If you have heard *no*, you have just spoken to the wrong person.' Start with: 'I would like to speak to the person responsible for...' – it is usually the manager or supervisor. Be firm – you want the right person.
2 'This is not what I was expecting, I would like my money back' or, 'I'm not satisfied with how this fits and would like to exchange it' or, 'I would like to talk to you about the bad customer service I received today and I would like an apology from the person concerned' or, 'My dress was stained by your server who spilled wine on it and I would like you to pay for it

to be dry-cleaned.' A clear opening position from you and a statement of what you want will yield better results.

3 Be firm, keep the same confident tone, full eye contact. 'I'm not satisfied with your answer/solution.' Repeat what you want the outcome to be again in the same, cool tone. If you still don't get satisfaction, insist on speaking to a higher authority. If they are not there, get their name and make an appointment to see them or get a direct phone number. Don't leave without the details of the people you have been dealing with so far, so that the next person knows the full story and the people you have dealt with and the dates. It is important to have the chronology. Save any receipts or paperwork. Continue to be cool-headed and fair. You want a solution, you don't want to go away angry.

I hope you don't have to go this far. Most businesses know we have choices and can spend our money elsewhere. The key is persistence. Most people don't bother, or they give up.

Structure 4: saying no

Not being able to say no is no laughing matter. It is a spiral that is difficult to get out of because it feels good to say yes and the people around you start to depend on it. And depend on it, and depend on it.

 case study Geoff: the yes-man

My partner's friend Geoff is the big brother in a large family. His father died when the children were all very young, so Geoff became by default the grown-up male of the family, and as a youngster started assuming a lot of responsibility for his brothers and sisters. Some 30 years later, his siblings still rely on him to 'save the day'. I have been at a picnic on a Sunday with Geoff when he has been called on his mobile and asked if he could pick up a niece or nephew from soccer practice, or to drop everything in favour of one task or another. He always finds a way of complying, or agonises over not being able to do something.

I decided to have a chat with Geoff about this privately one day when he was lying on the sofa exhausted, 'hiding' at our place. I wanted him to put the years of habit and feelings of guilt aside. I had him practise the following:

1 Ask yourself if the request is reasonable – if there is any doubt, you probably don't want to do it.
2 Most of the time, you need to get more information and clarification. Ask for it! Sometimes to get you to say yes, people will leave out unsavoury bits of information. Understand exactly what they are asking for, and why they feel they need to. (In Geoff's case, was he the only solution they had or did they just not want to interrupt the fun they were having doing something else?)
3 Resist the urge...if you don't want to do it at this point, say no.
4 Don't apologise. This is an important point. Don't say, 'I'm sorry but...'. It's not your problem, so don't own it by apologising for it. Also, if you do, you give a signal to the other person that you are possibly open to persuasion.
5 Instead, say no, clearly. Then pause briefly. Follow with your explanation of why you don't want to do it. If you want to or you care, help the person find another solution.

It was important that Geoff and I rehearsed these situations. I thought also that it was good to 'take him by surprise', so we agreed that I would call him on the phone and role-play when he wasn't expecting it. We also did this around the dining table, on walks in the park, and while out shopping. In fact anywhere, which is usually where it happened to him! I know now that it is working, because he is saying no to me more as well.

Being 'in the NO'

The key to saying no effectively is to say it once and say it well. Below are some tips on ways to begin sentences or answer requests:

- 'It is my policy not to...'
- 'I decided a long time ago never to...'
- 'No, thank you.'
- 'I would prefer not to.'
- 'No, thanks, that doesn't suit me right now.'
- 'No, I'm not interested.'
- 'No. I have other plans.'
- 'No. Can I help you find an alternative?'

My partner is always impressed at how I am able to get rid of unwanted telemarketers and door-to-door salesmen. Bless him, he would have us up to our ears in sponges and magazine subscriptions if he went unchecked. He hates the tension of these kinds of interactions. I use the 'three times you're out' method. It allows me to be civil to the other person and still get rid of them:

Knock knock

'Hi – I'm selling magazine subscriptions for my school fundraiser. Would you like to have a look?'

'No, thanks, I'm not interested.'

'I have some of the most popular titles, you might enjoy reading *House and Home*. Fifty per cent off the retail price.'

'No, thanks, I'm not interested.'

'But I want to win my school competition and if I sell one more subscription I will be able to take my elderly mum on her first holiday.'

'No thanks, I'm really not interested. Good luck.' *Close the door.* Well done.

The same approach works with telemarketers. Be pleasant but firm – it is aggravating, but remember you don't have to pick up the phone, you don't have to buy anything, and you have the power to hang up.

Being confronted: a look at the other side...

Our most unpleasant experiences to do with being confronted often come from being taken by surprise. Someone may disagree with you, verbally attack you, criticise you, or just be plain nasty.

No matter what your confrontation style or experience, you can handle it.

One of the hardest things to do when someone is confronting you is to remain calm and objective. It takes practice and courage. I would like you to think about it another way. As Miguel Ruiz says in his inspirational book *The Four Agreements*, 'Don't take anything personally.' Taking things personally is actually the maximum expression of selfishness, because we make the assumption that everything is about 'me'.

As I have said before, what others say about you (good or bad) or how they feel, is their problem not yours. Nothing they say or think is really about you. It follows then that you are not responsible for the actions of others, just for your own actions.

With this in mind, you can have the courage to be objective while being confronted.

You must then have the determination to understand the perspective of the person you are dealing with. If you know

where they are coming from, you will improve your chances
of diffusing the tension and learning the real reason for the
confrontation.

Dealing with criticism

Most of us find it hard to deal with criticism, even if it is fair.
The rule here is, if it isn't fair, don't take it personally. If it is
fair, don't take it personally, but acknowledge it and consider
it a gift.

Criticism isn't 'clean' or fair if it is laced with judgement.
For example, 'You said you would call and cancel dinner with
Joe and Sue and you haven't done it yet' is fair. 'You are trying
to get out of it so I'll have to do it, aren't you?' is judgemental.
'You're right, I haven't done it. I'll do it right after lunch today'
is a positive response, acknowledging that the criticism is fair.
Don't bite if the other person exaggerates or adds a judgement
call. Take the high road, stay calm and in control of the
situation.

If the criticism is personal in nature, seek first to understand.
Ask a question to clarify, so you will either get a real answer
and can deal with the problem or you will discover that the
person is just being obnoxious and has no real problem at all.

So, for example:

'Your friend Mark is always so patronising to me when we all
go out together, and you never defend me – you are too busy
having fun.'
'In what way do you feel patronised by him?'

Once you have established it is not just a case of paranoia or
insecurity, or a way to pick a fight, you can explore the details
of the problem, and work towards resolving it:

'Does he always behave that way to you?'
'Why do you feel that I let you down – what is it you would like me to do or say, and do you think it would help?'

The important thing in this example is not taking the criticism at face value. Before jumping to defend yourself (in other words, taking it personally), and thereby fuelling the confrontation, you need to work out why this criticism is being levelled at you, and what is behind it. Seeking to understand before you respond will be your protection against things getting worse. There are many ways of responding to an accusation or confrontation, and finding the most appropriate response in each instance is essential if misunderstandings and grievances are to be resolved.

Responding appropriately in the moment – the accompaniment to not taking it personally

As this chapter has highlighted, whatever the reason, the way you respond to someone who confronts you is important in contributing to how well things turn out. As witnessed in the example above, you have the intention to understand the context, but what if the other person is just being mischievous, mean or unfair? Maybe they just want to unsettle you, or are jealous, or showing off. If so, here are ways to deal with it:

- Ignore it – sometimes they may be just winding you up. Take away their power.
- Use humour to defuse the tension – be clear that you are not laughing at them but rather finding a funny side to the situation.
- Walk away – but be careful because it is hard to walk back in. Be sure you really want to do this.
- Subtly let them know you are aware of what they are doing – by holding eye contact, pausing, commenting on whether their behaviour is appropriate or necessary, even asking them to stop.

▪ Stall for time – give yourself space to think about your response. It could be minutes or hours or days. Sometimes having some time to gather your thoughts before responding can help a lot. Don't be afraid to say that is what you need.

▪ Ask a positive question – you want to understand why they are saying or doing something. This doesn't mean sarcasm, so be careful of your tone. It is a genuine question, phrased in a positive way to get a clear answer. It may take them by surprise: 'Phil, I'm interested in how you feel. Why are you so angry?'

▪ Tit for tat – give as good as you get. Take the moral high road here – if someone does something underhanded or mean, you don't need to descend to that level. Rather, if someone is tough, be tough back.

However, I find that most questions or comments originate from plain old misunderstandings.

If someone confronts you with a tough question or something you don't understand

We have all had a situation where we are asked something we don't know the answer to or are confronted about something we don't understand. Someone asks something in an aggressive or confusing way – where do we start?

I have found over the years that when there is a genuine misunderstanding between two people, the answer lies in one of three places.

1 *The missing link*

This is when the person who is confronting you is actually missing a vital piece of the puzzle and doesn't know it. They are genuinely confused because they don't know what you are talking about. They may look bemused or lose interest in what you are saying. Or perhaps dispute something that seems obvious to you. The problem may lie in missing information – they didn't read the article or see the programme or receive the memo. The whole thing doesn't hang together for them. It doesn't make sense, so they start to get agitated.

I remember vividly a meeting that was going on for hours into the late evening. Everyone was getting tired and cranky and we didn't seem to be progressing towards a close because of a disagreement between two people about a minor detail in the contract. Close to midnight, one of the assistants realised that they were dealing with two different contracts – only one of them had been updated with the right budget figures. When the missing information was suddenly available, we could all agree and go home.

If this happens to you:

■ Don't be shy about asking a question when the answer may be obvious to you, to check other people's understanding.
■ Listen for clues in your conversation. If you hear objections or questions like 'I don't understand why this is relevant to me'; 'How much will it cost?'; 'Where did you hear about this idea?'; 'Who told you?'; 'How did this happen?', then it may give you an indication that they are missing the point!
The way to remedy the confusion is easy: after identifying it, provide the missing information. It is such a common occurrence to both speak and listen without full information or the right information that it's a wonder we get on at all!

2 *The information clash*
This is when there is plenty of information but the other person's definition or understanding is different from yours. It often happens when the context is unclear or assumed. I was at

a lunch once where two people were talking about gun control. The discussion was getting more and more tense. I couldn't resist joining in and clarifying what I was hearing. It turned out that one was defining gun control as 'ownership of any firearms should be illegal', while the other saw it as 'there should be restrictions on some models'. They thought they were discussing the same issue, but they were defining it quite differently.

Again, listen for clues in your conversation.

My favourite example happened to me recently while I was trying on some jeans in a fancy clothing store, with a very young employee fashionista trailing behind. I tried on three pairs and thought that they were all a little too snug around the hips. I chatted to the assistant about preferring 'well-fitting jeans', something that flattered my figure. She said she knew exactly what I should have, and came back with several more for me to try on. After 30 depressing minutes of trying on overly tight jeans, I asked her if there was anything else in the store that would fit. She didn't understand, she said, because anything else would be too big and fit too loosely. I finally realised that she thought 'well-fitting' meant 'very tight' whereas I had meant 'a bit looser'. When this happens:

- Aim to clear up the misunderstanding or change the emphasis.
- Be prepared to listen with full attention to what the other person wants to know.

The information may be there but not in the form they want it or there may simply be a misunderstanding: 'Oh, you are talking about a lunch meeting. You mean including eating or just a meeting between twelve and two o'clock?'

3 *The values clash*

This happens when your personal values or priorities are different on the subject, or you just don't agree. You can spot this when the same objection or question keeps coming up or someone keeps agreeing or disagreeing to the same thing. It usually also means that you have not addressed a value or need that is important to the other person in a way they need you to.

My friend Julia works in a particularly male-dominated specialist area of engineering and, when she started a new job, found it very difficult to fit in with her colleagues. After a painful peer review she consulted me and we realised that her 'not fitting in' was less about being a woman (okay, it was a lot) and more about her not socialising in the pub after work. Julia is an award-winning athlete who spends her time after work and at weekends training for marathons or triathlons, and she simply hadn't understood the culture of sharing confidences and getting to know each other over a beer. Once she worked this out, she found that one night a month with the guys meant a lot to them, and helped to build the relationships she needed in order to work effectively.

Confrontation, in all its forms, is part of the rhythm of everyday life. Learn to recognise it for what it is and respond to it appropriately. It is a friend in disguise.

chapter **five**

if you don't ask,
you don't get

Do you recall some of those times in life when someone
says something to you and only later do you realise how
prophetic it is? Late one night, my friend and colleague
Betsy and I were in a critical planning meeting with a
client, and I was beginning to feel we were getting bogged
down. Then Betsy asked a question that I hadn't thought
of asking, and probably wouldn't have dared to ask even
if I had. Kind of like the emperor's new clothes, it was
something that was potentially volatile that needed to be
asked, right then or never. In this case the question was
as simple as, 'Why do you feel that way?' but the answer
we got was ground-breaking, and shifted the direction
that the planning was taking.

Later, in the car on the way back to the office, I told
Betsy I had enjoyed that moment, admired her for doing
it and thanked her for her guts. She replied, 'Well, if you
don't ask you don't get.'

Betsy and I were business partners for many years and I learned
a lot from being around her. She has a particular strength that
sets her apart from anyone else, and that contributes to her
success as a business person, mother, wife and friend.

Betsy is a fearless asker. This means that when she can see
that a client would be better off with our services, she asks for
the business. When she needs help or clarification on
something, she asks for it. When she isn't happy about
something, she asks if she can sit and talk it through. She would
ask for the seat she wanted in a restaurant, or to have her food
prepared to her liking. She would ask for more salary if she felt
it was justified. A good deal of what she asks for ends up
benefiting others. She asks to get involved in her son's school
governing board, her church activities and charitable events.

Before you think she sounds like a graduate from the school of super-mums, she's not. She certainly makes a sport out of doing a lot, but the crucial difference here is that for the most part she chooses what she does and does not do.

Her willingness to ask seems to create a snowball effect – the more she asks and gets, the more successful she becomes at asking and getting. The net result is that she is successful at getting much more of what she wants.

Betsy is rare. Most of us recognise our Betsys as being in possession of a more direct style than the rest of us, comfortable with making statements and conclusions in everyday language, and having the confidence to express desires or ideas.

The forces that shape why we are comfortable or uncomfortable about asking are often difficult to pin down. Many say, 'It's just not me' or, 'I feel like I am intruding if I ask' or, 'I didn't even think to ask.' I often find that people can be clear about what they want/need to ask for but block their chances of receiving it because of a deep-seated belief that they don't really deserve what they are asking for. This can be due to shyness (so you avoid asking), a sense of unworthiness or lack of self-esteem (so you avoid asking), fear (so you avoid asking), or some other reason (so you avoid asking).

The need to improve your asking skills often becomes apparent in a crisis, or when you are facing an extreme situation. Perhaps you are running the risk of losing a major client or relationship, or you need to keep on top form while your business is on a winning streak. You may be on the brink of promotion or have failed to secure the job you want. Or you are stuck in a rut or a relationship that you can't see your way out of. Maybe asking is a skill you should consider working on.

There are two aspects to being able to ask, and each needs to be present in order for asking to work in an effective and meaningful way. The first is to do with your attitude and commitment to asking for what you need or want, and the second concerns the tools you need to do it.

Our attitudes and willingness are shaped by our life experience – family, culture and personal experience. These influences are very powerful, and drive our responses and preferences in ways of which we are not always aware. A client of mine asked me to investigate why they were losing business little by little (both margin and revenue) after a major and positive restructure of their service offering. After some meetings with his senior team – the guys (as it happens, they were all guys) responsible for implementing the new offering – I realised what was happening. The revamping meant an increase in prices as well as a need to get 'more of the wallet' (that is, more of the total amount of money a client was spending), and this meant the team had to ask clients to spend more money with them. It turned out they were so uncomfortable with having to ask for new business from their existing relationships that they made themselves 'busy' with other types of work – finding excuses not to have the new conversation with the client, or, even worse, visiting the client, not asking for the business and reporting it as 'the client is not interested'. No one involved in the restructuring had asked the team how they felt about implementing it. The only clue was the loss of revenue, and although that could have triggered a number of responses from the company, it didn't evoke the absolutely key question – asking the team if they were okay asking! The irony was wonderful. Asking was the answer.

Each member of the implementation team had his own reason for being uncomfortable with the situation, but the theme was consistent. They had long-standing personal relationships with people they felt uneasy asking for new business. They thought it was somehow undignified and culturally unacceptable. Nothing was going to change their behaviour unless we could change their attitude towards this, and show them an acceptable way to approach the client.

The solution included open and detailed discussions, backed up by lots of evidence, about the relevance of the new offering to the client ('They will be better off with it'). It also included coaching with individuals about the different ways they could construct conversations that worked for both them and the client – in other words, how to have a new conversation that felt like the old ones. After a few weeks, they started having successful meetings and they realised they were 'helping the client to buy a better solution' rather than acting like door-to-door salesmen (which is how they almost universally interpreted 'asking').

So what is going on inside your head when you don't want to ask for something? Do you recall being told, 'If wishes were horses beggars could ride' or, 'If you have to ask for it then you shouldn't have it'? Why should it be easier to believe statements like this than, 'If you don't ask you don't get' or, 'Ask and it will be given'? I say that you can choose a positive commitment to asking and, as a result, more often get what you want and need.

Asking is not the dark underbelly of anything. Nor is it the opposite of humility or courteousness or respect. Asking is a crucial tool for understanding. The old adage 'Seek first to understand' is facilitated more by asking than by anything else.

There is another important dimension to asking, and that is your level of commitment to what you are asking for. Think about commitment as a focus – a vibe, an energy around you that embodies your true desire for something to happen.

Here's a promise – asking with the right amount of commitment gets you better results. When you ask for what you want and it is aligned with the right level of commitment, asking takes on its real magic for you.

Put another way, when you focus your attention on a particular thought (I can ask or I can't ask), or feeling (I want it or I don't want it), and you keep reiterating and reinforcing it, you will bring about changes to your personal experience.

Think about the example I gave you earlier – those guys who put their effort and energy and commitment into believing that asking was a dirty word. It became exactly that for them: revenue dropped and the 'culture of asking' became the 'anti-culture of asking'. When they started practising a different approach, combined with a different belief/commitment, revenue started to climb and they started having more fun doing what they were paid to do!

So, now on to the other important component. What skills and tools do you need in order to get better at asking?

Over the past twenty years, not one client has come to me and told me that they needed help with asking per se. No one has ever said, 'I need to improve how I ask for what I want' or, 'I need to ask more often' or, 'I want to figure out how to get more and better insight' or, 'I don't think I am asking the right questions.' Many people just need a curiosity injection – they don't make a habit of asking, seeking advice or direction. They may ask questions to confirm what they already know. It's not always arrogance (although often it is), but rather a lack of skill in asking, and not being aware of its inherent benefits.

case study George: trying hard
instead of trying right

George was considered very talented and loyal to his employer. He
did everything right, and had been in his job for a number of years.
His work demonstrated that he could handle a promotion, but he
kept missing out. His direct boss had become frustrated because
he had tried twice to promote George to the next level, but kept
getting push-back from his colleagues.

I met George alone to discuss the feedback with him. In our
sessions together, the challenge very quickly revealed itself. When
he spoke about himself or when he was sharing insights about
himself or his work, statements came out sounding like questions.
His tone went up at the end of sentences, which made it sound as
if he was seeking approval. Combined with this, he would giggle
quietly whenever he said something important, as if to play down
its significance. In meetings with others, I noticed that he added
questions to the end of his statements, such as, 'Don't you think?'
or, 'Isn't it?' or, 'Doesn't it?' He would smile a lot while asking
others to carry out important tasks, and his requests for assistance
were indirect. Instead of stating directly what he wanted a team
member to do – 'This report must be finished by noon tomorrow.
Please would you take it over and complete it' – he would say,
'There is a lot of work to do to complete this before noon
tomorrow. I am struggling with it and need some help.' As a result,
others might agree tentatively in the meeting and not follow it up.
George would then put off asking until he was so frustrated or
resentful that when he did, he came across as angry or emotional.

Physically, George tended to stand slightly off balance. His
posture was distracting: shoulders tilted and head a little turned
away from the centre of the conversation, making him appear shy.
When he was making a point, he distracted the listener with
gestures that looked as if he was dismissing his own ideas.

All these things made others feel George lacked gravitas and confidence – skills coveted by senior managers. He was smart, experienced and capable, but trapped by his doubting of his own abilities.

We started by changing the way George spoke to others. He practised using more direct language, by focusing clearly on what he wanted, and spelling it out in the fewest words possible. We also practised some subtle physical adjustments that aligned his physical posture more closely with the importance of his messages.

A tip that worked beautifully for him came simply from replacing, 'Could you help me?' with, 'Would you help me?' Doing this invoked a very different response from co-workers. In essence, it removed the emotion from his requests. Sometimes 'could' can be perceived as a question about someone's abilities, whereas 'would' is focused on willingness.

Another subtle change we brought about was to make him practise statements without the follow-on 'tag' questions. In my experience, there is always a particular physical tic that accompanies the tendency to use tag questions. In George's case, it was embedded in his off-balance posture. We straightened his body to balance his weight on both feet, and relaxed his shoulders. This was very difficult for him at first because he said he felt 'exposed' when he was facing someone so squarely. But he persisted and it soon became easier. The dismissive gestures seemed to disappear without much effort once he changed this posture, as did the tag questions.

We also made a long list of the things I had heard him say that needed to be stated more directly. Here are a few – I made him practise out loud and role-play them with me before using them with others:

I don't think we have talked about this enough
became
Would you schedule a meeting so we can talk about this in more detail?

Sorry, I don't think it is going to work
became
I have considered the idea and I am not interested in pursuing it

Can you get this done by close of play tomorrow?
became
Please finish this by 5pm tomorrow

I don't have time to finish this and I think I need some help
became
Would you handle the completion of this proposal?

In our conversations, he would often use references from his personal life, so I asked if he would like to practise some more affirmative ways of asking in an outside-the-office context. He was excited by this idea, so we explored some examples:

Why can't I find a girlfriend?
became
I want a wonderful relationship

I'm stuck in a dead-end job
became
I want to be doing a job I love

I keep meeting neurotic women
became
I want to meet a wonderful woman who shares my values

I hate being broke all the time
became
I want to be financially secure

I am so stressed all the time
became
I want to relax and enjoy life more

Practising this more direct and positive way of communicating with others, and seeing the results, gave George a greater feeling of confidence, but he was still bogging himself down with attitude blocks arising from his habit of self-doubt. We constructed some powerful affirmations for him – some inner thoughts to focus on as he applied his new behaviours. Here are some examples from George's private meditation list:

- I intend to attract what I want and stop thinking about what I don't want.
- I intend to feel confident and strong, communicating my ideas to others.
- I intend to attract stimulating and worthwhile projects that satisfy my desire to be creative.
- I intend to build authentic relationships with those around me.

George wanted to attract more confidence and success in his life – not to feel so doubtful in work and personal situations. He needed to stop thinking about what he didn't want and to focus on what he did want. He was responsive to the idea of visualising the success he desired, as well as the responses of the people around him and the feeling of confidence. This technique doesn't work for everyone, but in George's case the exercises and role-plays enabled him to rehearse being the person he wanted to be.

The most recent news I had of George was that he had found a new girlfriend and had left his job for a better position at a competitor firm! Well done, George – whatever the reason, something changed for the better for you.

Now for the essential toolkit for everyday skills. What do you need to be able to do in order to add firepower to asking, and make it really work for you? Simple. Some skills. There is such a thing as a well-structured, appropriate and well-timed question. It is the sort I referred to earlier with Betsy. However, most people aren't aware that they are not technically good at asking questions, and often those who think they are good, aren't. As a consequence, the answers they get from people are not as good as they could be.

There is a lot of information out there about the classic types of questions you can ask in certain situations, based on the kind of answer you are looking for. However, in my years of working with people I have found that there are really only four you should bring to the top of the list and practise. They are the amulet of asking, if you like. They facilitate a quicker path to understanding others and getting the answers you want and need.

First, a general word about the power of good questions. Good questions will bring you closer to your listener. More than that, they enable a proper exchange to take place between two people. For your listener, asking proves you are listening. Asking good questions means you are building a rapport. This is when you get access to the real reasons why someone feels the way they do and to what it is that drives their opinions and decisions. They will gain new insight into their own situation, and so you can get a clearer picture of what their needs may be. A bounty of benefits!

You can see that there are a number of reasons why you should want to become technically better at asking questions. Let's focus on the four most important types: I call them

- the combo
- the follow-up
- what, which, why
- the hypothetical

The Combo

This is when you can consciously combine open- and closed-ended questions to keep conversation flowing. It creates a wonderful rhythm that allows an exchange between you and the other person – each giving and then taking. Open questions are great if you want to explore thoughts and feelings and attitudes and to invite longer, more revealing answers. Be sure to ask them in a friendly and interested way.

Open questions start with words such as 'How' or 'Why'. What do you think about...? What are your feelings about...? Would you give me an example of...? Would you elaborate on...? What is your opinion on...? Tell me about...

Closed questions work wonders for getting specific information and brief, pointed answers. They usually start with 'What', 'Which', 'Would you', 'Do you'. For example: 'So, do you come here often?' (answer); 'What do you do?' (answer); 'How long have you been doing that?' (answer); 'Do you enjoy it?' (answer) etc. When? Where? How many? How much? How long? Who? What? Too many of these can feel like an interrogation. Yes No Yes No Yes No. If you ask a closed question to someone who is shy or usually doesn't talk a lot, you are likely to get a very brief answer. If, on the other hand, you meet a friendly, talkative person, you may get a longer answer. There are exceptions to the rule – I have found myself sometimes using closed questions in an attempt to keep someone from talking too much, to no avail.

Open and closed questions combined often feature in those conversations where you suddenly look at your watch and it is way past your bedtime – how did that happen? Time flies when you are doing the Combo! The most common mistake people make is to ask too many of one or the other – leading either to aimless verbal wandering or to an interrogation. Sometimes people need a little encouragement to play along with you. So a good example might look like this:

(Closed) 'John, has it really been two years since I've seen you?'
'Yes. Hard to believe.'
(Open) 'How have you been?'
'Fine really.'
(Open) 'I remember you were just starting a new job at the gallery. How is it going?'
'Good. Still there.'
(Open) 'Tell me more about it.'

Be careful – another common mistake with Combos is to ask multiple questions all in one breath without waiting for the answers: 'Hi. How nice to see you! How have you been? How are your kids, hey is your son happy at his new school – how long has he been there – I heard the other day the school just got an award for scholastic achievement, did you hear about it?'

Hmmm, where do I start?

The Follow-up

This technique is very important because its main purpose is to encourage the other person to keep talking, or to share more. Of all the question techniques, it is the one that takes people most by surprise. It is also the one that often gets passed over because the best opportunity to use follow-up questions is when no one wants to say anything. In the example I gave at the start of the chapter, Betsy had first asked an open-ended question: 'How do you feel about the agreed timing?' The client then gave a long answer about how they felt it was not the right time. Betsy's killer follow-up question – 'So, why do you feel that way?' – opened a conversation that changed the tide of everything we were doing with that particular client.

Follow-up questions can be difficult because when we need them most, there is often a lot of tension – positive or negative – that may block the natural response. This tension might be due to you needing to probe something that could be embarrassing, or to finding yourself wanting to quickly correct someone or judge. The patience it takes to ask a follow-up question means that you are going to suspend judgement and try to seek more information. The other person often gives you clues that they want you to ask a follow-up question – usually by their choice of words. For example, if someone says, 'I'm not sure the colour is right' they are inviting a follow-up question in order to expand and explain. Unless you ask, you won't know if they like the colour but not the tone, or if they really wanted bright purple. The key is to follow up by asking for clarification on a word you don't understand: 'Would you clarify for me what you mean by that?' or, 'I'm not sure what you mean by that, can you tell me more?' Or, if they have used a particularly emotional word: 'Tell me more about how you feel about it' or, 'I don't understand completely, please tell me a little more.'

The magic words, 'Could you go into that a bit more?' or, 'Tell me more about that' can be music to someone's ears.

What, which, why

I have chosen this third technique because it represents the nearest thing to an asking 'plan' that most of us need to have. It is particularly useful in situations where you must be relevant and persuasive. Preparing your series and order of questions is a good idea if you stand to gain or lose a lot in a certain set of circumstances. This technique is a 'drill down', and is likely to get you access to the real reasons why someone is feeling or doing something. Level one is understanding the 'what' – what someone is doing, what are the critical elements, what are the reasons, what are the criteria. In other words, the things you need to know about what the situation IS.

The next level of drill down is understanding someone's priorities. The 'which' allows you to do this. Of the things you have been discussing, which are the most critical or important or interesting or pressing or stimulating or scary? This is when you start to gain an insight into the information you have received in the 'what'.

The 'why' is the holy grail of asking. If you can reach this stage, you can understand what is truly motivating the other person. This is where you get meaning and values. Here are two examples of how the 'what, which, why' order of asking might work in practice:

- What is it that motivated you to move to a new city?
- Which aspects of it are most important to you in order to feel as though you are really settled?
- Why is that so important? How do you feel about it?

- What do you think are the key success factors for this project?
- Which of those do you think are the most important?
- Why do you think that?

This form of asking doesn't usually happen one line after the other. It may evolve over the course of one or many conversations – primarily because the real answers often require you to have some kind of earned trust before you get access to them. The skill is in staying focused and being ready when the clue is presented to you.

Forget about 'getting to yes' – the successful person of the future is the one who is 'getting to why'. I believe anyone who can grasp the power of bringing 'why' into their repertoire will gain access to the real reasons people feel the way they do, and consequently understand the broader considerations behind decision-making.

The Hypothetical

I love this type of enquiry because it throws form out of the window. It asks for a prediction. I recommend you use this in two situations: if you have reached a block and you or the other person can't really think of anything else to say; or if you just want to have fun and explore possibilities.

Often we know the answers to the most problematical questions facing us. Try asking yourself: 'If you knew the answer, what would it be?' I dare you! You will probably be able to blurt out the answer. I have done this many times with clients when it seemed we had reached a point where we could go no further. Of course sometimes there is no answer yet and you need to wait for it, but often if you try this you will surprise yourself. Or it may leave you thinking for a few days. Or suddenly bubble up an answer you hadn't even thought of. This form of asking seems to link to a part of the brain where we store the notion of possibility. Try it and wait for the first thing that pops into your head – or ask someone and wait patiently for the answer. Some examples:

- 'If you had a wish list, what would be on it?'
- 'Why are you going to be able to achieve it?'
- 'It is now one year from now, what does it look like?'
- 'So, why are you going to win the business?'
- 'Why will you succeed?'

A hypothetical question is based on the imaginary or possible. Since I think that anything that is imagined is possible, this is a very powerful tool!

These four question types will get you through 90 per cent of situations where it is important that you learn, clarify, understand and build relationships. Decide what you want or need to know, on the most appropriate order or series of questions, and which types of questions are best suited for the task. Then practise them. Doing so will raise your awareness and ensure you continue to improve. Thinking about it isn't enough.

Align these skills with the suitable level of commitment to what you want to ask for or ask about, and you have a formidable force at the tip of your tongue.

chapter **six**

listen to learn

I want to share a story with you that sounds a little like something out of a Disney movie, but it really did happen to me.

Some years ago, I was walking along the street in downtown Manhattan, rushing between meetings, when I looked down and saw that there was a crumpled-up piece of paper stuck to my shoe. I had my arms full with a computer bag and folders, and tried to get it off by shaking my foot, but it just stuck there. As I was hopping around, trying to scrape the paper off my foot, I found that I had hopped myself into the street. Before I was aware of what was going on, a man had grabbed me and pulled me swiftly and firmly out of the way of an oncoming delivery truck going at high speed and trying to clear a red light. After I got over my initial shock and thanked him profusely, I finally bent down to remove the piece of paper from my shoe.

Out of curiosity, I unfolded the wet blob to see some blurry phone numbers and scribbles, along with a faintly visible message: Listen to Learn... I didn't think much about it (except that it might make a good bumper-sticker), but as there wasn't a litter bin nearby, I put the piece of paper in my bag and continued on my way.

Years later, the same piece of paper appeared again, at the bottom of an old bag. It happened to be an emotionally dark time in my life – I was finalising my divorce and negotiating a tense, make-or-break contract with my long-term business associates that didn't look as if it was going to end well.

I smiled to myself and reflected on the last time I had seen this little piece of paper, grateful for small mercies and random acts of kindness.

However, at that moment on the floor of my empty apartment, this message actually meant something else very important to me. My business and personal lives were complicated by the fact that I did not listen very well.

I had spent the previous 20 years helping people to communicate better and extolling the virtues of being a good and effective listener. I had been confident that I was following my own advice and understood those closest to me. But what I was learning from the mess of my current situation was that I wasn't listening fully to what people were saying to me, nor was I paying attention to the facts. It was as if my buttons were stuck on 'transmit'. I was on my path, living my life my way. I thought I knew the questions and the answers. I felt I understood everyone's motivations and needs and was serving them well. Wrong.

After this wake-up call, I made a sincere and focused effort to practise better listening (and I'll talk more about how to do this later in the chapter). The journey has been difficult but fascinating, and I have discovered things I never expected. With my improved listening, interesting things have started to happen. My personal relationships have become richer and more rewarding. I have been asked to be involved in more varied and complex work. I find it easier to work with different types of people. I have even attracted a publisher who has enabled me to approach the creative process in a new and exciting way.

Listening is defined by the International Listening Association (yes, there is one) as 'the process of receiving, constructing meaning from or responding to spoken and/or non-verbal messages'. In addition, real listening includes a 'willingness to gain another's perspective'. But my favourite interpretation comes from the composer Leonard Bernstein when he was asked, 'What is music?' He replied, 'Music is what happens between the notes.'

So, part science, part art.

In this chapter, I would like to focus on practical ways for you to identify how well you are listening in situations that may be important to you, and offer you some actions that, with a little reflection and some application, will enable you to become a better listener and begin to make changes for the better.

So why should you care about improving your listening? Well, listening is one of those things that you can spend your entire life not knowing you are mediocre at, and as a consequence not get access to the benefits it can bring to you and those around you. I think you should care because it is the skill that can move you forward in life most quickly and in the most interesting ways. You should care because listening helps you discern the true nature of a situation. Understanding what is really happening in the moment makes you agile, flexible, able to move on, and capable of responding to your world in the most powerful way.

Over the past ten years, there has been a lot of interest in listening, from the business world in particular. Tougher regulations and legal risks have meant that not listening can be costly. Organisations realise that in order to design, develop and launch products successfully they need to 'listen' to their customers. In order to stay in business, they need to know and understand their customers better than anyone else. In a world where ideas are hard to differentiate, the stakes are higher and there is so much vying for our attention that listening has become a valuable skill.

I have many clients who now count listening skills as key criteria they test for when they recruit board members and senior executives.

Listening is even good for your health. A recent study showed that when we are listening, our heart rate slows and our oxygen consumption is reduced. Through your willingness to gain another's perspective, you can help them get something off their chest and maybe see things a different way. Both of you can lower your blood pressure, reduce stress and improve each other's well-being.

Yeah, yeah, lovely, I hear you say. But I haven't yet met anyone who has ever made it their new year's resolution to become a better listener. If you have ever done this, hats off to you – you are rare.

Studies show that most people think they are good listeners, because they have been told so by someone, or because they don't interrupt others. Maybe you are the one everyone talks to, or confides in, or gossips to. Perhaps you allow others to talk more than you do in conversation. But saying nothing does not a good listener make!

The human body is hard-wired to listen. The obvious way is through our ears and eyes; however, listening also happens through touch, smell, feeling, temperature, pulse, rhythm and gut feeling, or intuition – and most of us have only one or two channels tuned in most of the time.

A friend of mine once described listening as being 'a problem of attention'. He said that we often find it difficult to listen because our attention is tied or fixed to too many things. We are often thinking of things we did yesterday or have to do later today or tomorrow. Partly consciously, partly unconsciously, much of our attention is somewhere else and it is difficult to free up on demand enough attention to listen to what is being said right now.

Listening requires willingness and enough available attention in the moment. A friend of mine once used a good analogy to explain this willingness, through the use of our other senses. For example, taste. In order to taste something new, you have to be willing to give it a try – you aren't sure if it will be pleasant or unpleasant, sour or sweet. Just as the new taste may change your attitude towards the food in front of you (I recently discovered that oysters were delicious, after years of turning them away), listening may change your thinking, opinions and attitudes. Listening should be as much a new and sought-after experience as tasting!

I still have to work constantly at listening. I had a breakthrough moment once, many years ago, when I commented to a colleague that my sessions were tiring me out a little too much – by the third or fourth hour with clients I was feeling stressed and needed a break. I was given feedback that changed and improved the way I listened. My colleague noticed that when I was working with clients, I leaned towards them with my head tilted slightly too far forwards and I was breathing shallowly and intermittently. This was causing me a lot of physical stress – hence the tiredness and weightiness. Armed with my new awareness, I took a step-by-step approach, starting with being conscious of the position of my head – more upright and relaxed; then my breathing – more regular and deeper in my belly; my posture – my spine straighter and my sitting bones level in the chair. This quickly led to a noticeable difference. I had far less fatigue, and went from three or four clients a day to easily managing eight. I listened more intently and had better, more helpful and relevant insights more quickly and, at the end of the day, I felt more energised.

In my experience, the best listeners have learned their big lessons through either curiosity, pain, necessity or humility. I would love to spare you the pain, so maybe we can supercharge your curiosity about listening, and see where it takes you.

Barriers to listening

We encounter listening barriers every day. If we know about them, we can control them or reduce their impact. Barriers to listening can be categorised into mental, emotional and physical barriers, and something I refer to as resting postures.

Mental barriers are things like:
- prejudice and judgement, and the knowledge you have about something (I'm the expert, why should I listen to these people?)
- how well or fast your brain processes the information (I wish she would speak a little slower so I could write my notes clearly)
- planning (I didn't know so-and-so was going to be at this meeting – how does he fit in?)
- structure of the message (I don't understand the problem – why is he proposing a solution?)
- control (I wish she would stop talking, this is my meeting)
- Time (we are running over time, we will never get to the point at this rate)
- observation (that person is sending strange signals – I don't know if I can trust him)

Emotional barriers can include things like:
- fear (I can't go back to the office without making a sale)
- lust (I wonder if he finds me as attractive as I find him)
- ego (I can't believe he thinks he knows more than me, I'll show him)
- greed (if I feign indignation, maybe I can get a better price out of him)
- self-consciousness (I wonder if they can tell I don't know a lot about this – I hope they can't see me blushing)
- doubt (do I deserve to be here – what if we can't get this completed?)

Physical barriers can be anything in your environment that acts as a distraction:

- heat (this room is too hot, the sun is coming in through the window and boiling me)
- cold (I wish I had my scarf – it's freezing in here)
- physical discomfort (ugh, these trousers are too tight)
- arousal (you figure it out)
- noise (oh no, the builders next door – not now)
- hunger (when's lunch?)

If you have ever tried to listen to someone while you needed to use the bathroom, you know what I mean.

Mental, physical and emotional barriers are always present. These are the things you are thinking about, or feeling or doing, instead of listening fully. I attended a conference recently and during the coffee break got talking to some of the other participants. As we were discussing the speakers and the subject matter the conversation started to get very funny. One person remarked that one of the speakers looked like one of his early school teachers and he couldn't concentrate because he kept imagining her at the front of his classroom and remembering how he used to get his hands slapped for misbehaving. Another felt that one speaker didn't stick to his published subject and he was annoyed and could only think about what he wasn't saying. Another woman said she was sitting under an air-conditioning duct and could only think about how to keep warm.

Apply this to everyone in the room, and you have a typical situation. Each person is listening only as well as they can. The world places barriers to listening in front of us most of the time. Start by being aware of what these barriers are for you, and then notice what might be causing them for others. Maybe you jumped to a quick judgement about someone even before they opened their mouth, maybe someone triggered a memory and you feel emotionally distracted, perhaps you are hungry, tired or uncomfortable. If you are willing to take notice, you can 'park' the barrier or remove it entirely, in order to listen more fully.

Resting postures is the name I give to another type of physical barrier to listening, which is hidden inside our bodies. Each of us adopts about three resting postures that we use most of the time, particularly while listening. They vary wildly from person to person, but include:

* crossing your legs in a particular way while seated
* keeping your arms folded while listening
* shifting your weight on to one hip while standing
* turning your face at an angle to the person you are listening to
* moving around, pacing the room
* slouching your shoulders
* looking away often while someone is talking
* fidgeting

Think about your own repertoire: when you are seated, listening to one person or a small group, where is your weight situated? How are your shoulders – tense or relaxed? What is your breathing like? Do you tend to cross one leg over the other, or slouch on one side? Do you lean into the chair to your right or left? Imagine if someone was to imitate you, what would they do? The most common resting postures involve sitting low in the chair, legs crossed, head resting on the hand. How about when you are standing? Do you lean your weight on one hip and rest there? Is there a predominant handful of postures you adopt that you can identify? How are these postures affecting your ability to listen?

I am not saying that any of these postures are bad or good, but that I believe your ability to listen is affected by them. They are a kind of physical 'groove', a familiar position we settle into when listening (or speaking).

Let me give you an example.

I had a client whose typical resting posture was to sit with his knees and body facing away from his listener and his head on a slant, as if he was looking at the speaker suspiciously. He came to me because he had recently taken on some new duties at work. His company had introduced new rules about collaboration, so he had to facilitate new behaviours across a wide spectrum of people – replacing suspicion and protection of territory with openness and discussion – and his manager was concerned he didn't have the support of his colleagues.

I drew this posture to his attention and asked him to move and face me fully without tilting his head. Incredible! The feeling was so different. Face forward, relaxed, full attention, not suspicious. I still have to mention it to him because, without thinking, he goes back into the resting posture, but it has made a difference to how others feel about him.

Remember in Chapter One I talked about how your past experience, and the things that you have got used to, set up a muscle memory which is stored in your brain? Well, associated with that are all sorts of unnecessary tensions which could be getting in the way of you listening, acting like a block to being able to pay attention properly. If you want to change these tensions, first you have to be aware that they are there. Then you need to suspend your usual response to a situation – thus allowing you to make a better choice.

Suspending your response will improve your awareness. It takes only seconds – sometimes milliseconds – but it can break the stranglehold that the bad habits have over you.

So how do you identify these postures so you can suspend your response and stop yourself from adopting them? You need to observe yourself.

If you find that you always default to a particular posture, try another one and see how it makes you feel. Often the most useful (but uncomfortable) ploy is to do the exact opposite of what you normally do. If you are sitting forwards, try sitting back; if you are leaning to one side, lean to the other. Make it definite rather than subtle. After a month or so, you are likely to find that you can listen to the world around you in a very different way. If you have ever practised meditation, you probably remember how challenging it was when you first started to sit silently for half an hour. Your body felt uncomfortable, or stiff, or twitchy. It wasn't until you practised waiting through this discomfort that you were able to reap the rewards of meditation. Well, it's a bit like that with listening.

Given all these barriers, it might seem as though good listening is all but impossible to achieve. The good news is that most of the barriers relate to things you can control. If you can't – if you are unable to listen properly or alter the circumstances – you can at least decide to postpone the conversation. Sometimes it can be as simple as saying: 'I would like to be able to focus on our conversation. It's really noisy here, let's move' or, 'I can't concentrate until I get something to eat' or, 'I would like to discuss this when I have a bit more energy – can we do it in the morning?'

Listening styles

Let's now have a look at the most common listening styles. These represent a level of 'quality' of listening. None of them is right or wrong. It is when we get stuck doing one of them most

of the time or using one style in an inappropriate context that
we get into difficulties:

- listening to be polite
- listening to be right or confirm
- listening selectively
- listening 'with the lights on'

Listening to be polite

This style of listening is when you are 'present but not
accounted for'. You may be physically there – or on the other
end of the phone – and may even look as if you are listening.
You may nod, grunt, smile and show interest, but your intention
is to be polite, not actually to engage enough energy to listen.
You may remember very little except that a pleasant, if
meaningless, exchange has taken place. Conversations at most
cocktail parties, casual business meetings and chance encounters
fall into this category, as, unfortunately, do many of those you
have with your partner and kids when you're tired at the end
of the day. This style is to do with survival or coping for the
weary or uninterested. It is the style that is the easiest to get
away with – the listening equivalent of taking a nap.

Of course, sometimes you have to listen to be polite, for
survival's sake, and it can be the best option in some
circumstances – such as when you are jet-lagged, don't really
have anything to say, or just want to be there if only in person,
like the party you agreed to go to where you put in an
appearance to show willingness, then go home as soon as
possible. But listening to be polite can be habit-forming, which
means you run the risk of missing out on something interesting
or stimulating, or of not taking the opportunity to show
someone you care by really engaging.

I have a friend who is regularly invited to openings of
exhibitions and similar events. He really dislikes the social whirl,
and describes predictable small talk as 'having the same effect
as a sleeping pill' at the end of a long day. He has chosen to
make the most of his hours of enforced polite listening, so he
plays a game with himself to take his listening out of the realm
of mere politeness, and to create interest for himself. His
approach is to 'find something interesting in everyone' and ask
a question that makes both parties think about the answer.

He has four key opening questions that he rotates, the
intention of which is to get the other person talking about
something other than, 'What do you do?' or, 'How do you
know…?' or, 'Are you enjoying the event?' The questions are
designed to elicit more personal, and therefore interesting,
information early on in the conversation. The following are
examples of his questions:

- 'What did you like most about the exhibition (or whatever
subject)?' rather than, 'How do you like it?'
- 'If the organisers could have done one thing differently
tonight, what would it have been?' rather than, 'Would you like
another drink?'
- 'How did you develop an interest in (your subject)?' rather
than, 'What do you do?'

Next time you are in a potential 'listen to be polite' situation,
notice your posture and how you are holding your weight. If
you find yourself in a familiar resting position – weight fully on
one hip, slouching into a chair, shallow breathing, maybe
bouncing back and forth a little from toes to heel, or fidgeting –
do something different. Make yourself a little uncomfortable by
shifting to the other side or standing on both feet with equal

weight, weight slightly forwards on your toes, shoulders relaxed and tummy tucked in. Stay there for a moment and see how it feels. If you are seated, try to sit with the edge of the chair seat midway up your hamstrings, feet flat on the floor, spine relaxed but erect, shoulders relaxed. This is better if you are at a table – if not, lean back in the chair but keep your weight on both buttock cheeks, shoulders relaxed, chin positioned as if you are trying to hold an orange gently between your chin and chest. Don't exaggerate this, just think about keeping your neck and shoulders relaxed and spine erect, without throwing your head back. And don't forget to breathe...

Life is full of moments where we wish we were somewhere else. Often, though, these moments can provide us with a richness we never imagined – if we pay attention to them.

Listening to be right or to confirm

Many of us have a habit of wanting to be right. For some it is a vocation – subject-matter experts of all kinds are paid to be right (the problem being that they bring it home with them). Some cultures and belief systems value the strong, outspoken leader, the confident, definite person. But they can be so busy trying to be right or to leave a good impression that they don't hear what is actually going on.

People like this may well be right sometimes. Like a stopped clock – right twice a day.

This style is characterised by interruption. Either by breaking in with a yup, yup, yup and finishing someone's sentence for them, or by waiting only long enough to let them stop before jumping in to talk about how you agree, or have had an experience like that or know of something exactly the same. This style also 'interrupts' in the sense that the listener stops paying attention as soon as they have heard what they need in order to confirm what they were already thinking, and to start thinking about something else. Almost as if they have 'ticked the box'. You can see it in their body language. Eye contact disappears or is sporadic, and they may even start doing something else. Their body is often leaning forwards as they speak or listen.

I have seen a number of people who listen to be right – they can be 'in a rush and only want to hear what I need in order to qualify you as a buyer' salesmen, or the person who believes it is their duty to be right because 'that's what you pay me for', or someone who is desperate not to be found out as an impostor, or the blamers of the world – out to unearth every clue that you are victimising them. All types tend to push their weight forwards in the heat of the moment, with their chest up ready to pounce. The underlying motivation behind this listening behaviour is fear – whether it be fear of losing, fear of failing, fear of being wrong or of being seen to lack knowledge.

If you know such a person, asking them nicely to stop interrupting or to listen until you have finished may not be enough – you have tried that, right? If you haven't, go for that first: 'John, it distracts me from my train of thought when you interrupt me or finish my sentences. Would you please wait until I finish?' While it won't necessarily deal with the underlying problem, it will help them to be more aware of how you feel.

If you find yourself listening to be right or confirm, at the point you feel the need to say something while the other person is mid-sentence or mid-thought, resist the urge to interrupt. Just don't do it. Wait. Suspend your usual response – make a better choice. You'll get your chance to make your point, if it is still relevant, by the time the other person has finished. If they do get to finish, you will have created the impression that you are a generous listener and have done a good thing for them (they won't know of your internal struggle).

Or try this exercise. When you are in a discussion in a business or formal setting and have an urge to make your point while someone else is speaking, write it down so you won't forget it. Don't be tempted to confirm that what the other person has said tallies with what you think ('Oh, I agree, I think you are right' etc.) or take them off track to describe your experience. Just note down the point. I have lots of clients who have tried this, and been amazed to find that when they check their list at the end of a conversation, many of the points they wanted to make or comment on were never needed, or didn't add anything to the successful conclusion. Often a better outcome was reached when they didn't add their long list of 'confirmations'.

Another exercise is to practise active acknowledgement, validation and sharing while listening, but not adding your own commentary.

Acknowledgement refers to making small noises or gestures that coax or invite the other person to continue. Small grunts, hmmms, ah-has, ohs, nodding slightly or very softly spoken words like 'really' or, 'I didn't realise that'. However, we've all met the annoying person who grunts or exclaims through our conversation to the point of distraction, and that's not what I mean.

Encouraging the person talking to go on can also take the form of small acknowledgements when you want to let them know that you have understood and that there is no need to continue or repeat. Things like, 'I understand what you mean', 'Interesting', 'I'm with you'. They are fairly non-committal but have a positive impact on the flow of the conversation.

Validation means that when the person you are talking with contributes an idea or an alternative that you like, you aren't afraid to compliment them. Often people who listen to be right or confirm withhold compliments through either embarrassment or stinginess. Sometimes they just don't think to say anything in the moment (perhaps owing to a lack of practice and awareness). These validating comments might go along the lines of: 'That's a really good idea, I hadn't thought of that.'

Sharing signifies that while you are listening, you add a little bit of your own experience or viewpoint. Just a little bit – don't monopolise the conversation and shift the focus to yourself. (Remember we are trying to break that habit!) It might take the form of: 'I feel the same way about that' or, 'That has been my experience too.'

The habit of listening to be right or confirm is a hard one to improve. However, if you chip away at the impulse to interject, you'll realise that you can often get what you need without having to be right or even having to be the one who makes the point.

One last thing: you can try some slow, steady breathing before you enter a discussion. Clarify the objective in your mind (if there is one) and have the courage to let your points pass. You may win even more often than you used to!

Listening selectively

This style, which uses clues and cues, is a bit more subtle and refined and by nature calls for a degree of elegant efficiency. This is because you usually adopt it when you have some idea of the outcome you are seeking from the encounter – you have done some homework, so you have a good idea of the information you need to get or the insights to be gained on particular issues. On the downside, you may be so intent on finding out or confirming your information that you keep the conversation going down a particular path and miss something you weren't expecting. On the upside, this kind of conversation can help you learn what you'd like to know more quickly, because you are going in with a plan. Because you are well prepared, you are more likely to impress the other person and gain access to better quality information sooner.

Imagine, for example, that you are going for a new job in a different department. You know the job description and salary, but with a little research you find you have a few more issues to discuss with the interviewer before you can make a decision. These include the job's starting date (so that it aligns with your taking holiday beforehand), the opportunity for you to get access to an overseas posting (you've always wanted to work abroad) and whether there is management support for your part-time night courses (which means you have to leave by 6pm on Wednesdays without fail).

Once you are in the interview, listen for opportunities to explore these issues. During conversations, people give us clues and cues. A good analogy is to imagine you are driving down the road and see that you are coming to a set of traffic lights some distance away. Some of the tail lights in the distance are starting to appear red – the cars are braking. This is a clue that soon you will be slowing down, or possibly stopping. As you get closer to the intersection, the cars just in front of you are braking – this is your cue to stop. It's the same with language. As you are discussing aspects of the new job, you get a clue that it is going to require weekend work and some late nights. You listen some more and find out that it is seasonal and predictable. Your cue to ask about Wednesdays!

Selective listening – you need to know what you can give, but also what you can get.

Listening 'with the lights on'

When your intention is to really learn about the other person, you are non-judgemental and open on many levels – in other words, the lights are on, you are seeing clearly and hiding nothing. As I mentioned earlier, with a little practice we are capable of listening on many levels at the same time. As with anything, you have to want to do it first. You may know something or nothing about this person, but you and he/she are willing to take the time and energy to discover a deeper understanding. This usually means you are listening with more empathy, may not be so quick to judge, and have a feeling for what is important for the other person as well as yourself. You are making the effort to listen more completely. This style of listening usually takes a little more time and attention to put into practice. But it's time well spent. I have found in business over the years that the intention to listen this way can actually cut the time it takes to get deals and negotiations completed, because there is an interest in seeking the underlying reasons/motivations/feelings that may block success later on. It is also where the biggest gains come.

Some of the best listening experiences I have had have been with complete strangers (and new romances!). I know this sounds odd, but hear me out. Listening to learn requires that you listen to someone as if you don't know them. You listen generously, take time and are happy to go down unexpected pathways. You are curious. Your awareness is heightened. There is little or no judgement because there is no history and very little knowledge of your habitual responses. You are usually in a place where there may be the time to spare – a plane, a coffee shop, in a queue. It is the perfect place to practise this kind of listening. You may end up learning something about yourself, either by how you feel at the end of the conversation – refreshed, relaxed, energised – or because you see your own situation in a new way. You may even have gained a new insight into something.

This is an exciting challenge. Practise this with people you know, in both business and personal relationships. There is a bounty waiting to be mined, I promise.

Here are some of the characteristics of this listening to learn style. Do all of them and you are a saint. Some of them most of the time, you are human and you've got the picture!

- Judge the content, not the messenger or how they are carrying it out.
- Resist the urge to control the conversation.
- Own your accusations – keep it first person. 'I've heard such-and-such', not: 'They told me'.
- Don't get defensive or take things personally.
- Find something you like about the other person (yes, there is always something – look for it early, keep looking).
- Listen to the person as if you had never met them before.
- Try to separate what you know first hand from second or third hand (this is the difference between 'knowing' and 'knowing about').
- Don't interrupt. Listen on until the end even if you know what the other person is going to say; use follow-up questions – don't presume all has been said.
- Allow about 20 per cent more time for listening than you think is necessary. Sometimes it takes longer than you expect to get to the good stuff.
- Be sensitive – when people feel threatened it is natural to get defensive. You may see aggression, anger, competitiveness. Forgive, understand, adjust what you are doing. Keep going.

As you become more aware, good-quality listening will continue to be a challenge. The essence of it lies in your intention to listen. It is not an easy journey, but is an intensely rewarding one that takes practice every day.

You can make big changes in subtle ways. Observe, suspend your response, make a better choice, observe. Reflect. Begin again. Well done.

chapter **seven**

pay attention
to get attention

'Attention is the investment we make to gain reward,' said a wise friend. It makes sense, then, to pay attention to get attention. When I say 'pay attention', I am not talking here about the mere act of listening – that is all covered in the previous chapter. I mean really paying attention – engaging yourself, concentrating, focusing on the issues in hand.

The promise here is that there are tangible benefits for anyone if they learn to pay attention more fully to what they are doing.

I have asked many people if they know what it feels like to pay attention fully or what would be in it for them if they did it more. Most of the time, the answer is, 'I don't know, I don't think about it much.' Yet in my experience, needing to pay attention more fully is a problem that is common to all my clients, and can be the key that unlocks the door to any change they want to make.

After learning how to pay attention fully, clients have told me that they get through the day using less energy and with lower stress levels. Some have said that they are more productive and the quality of their work is better; others that they get a sense of well-being, relief, calm and satisfaction. In many cases they have improved their ability to build rapport and relationships.

So what do I mean by 'paying attention more fully' and why is it so important?

Think about the 100-metre sprint in the Olympics. As you watch the start, which of the runners do you think will win? The one who is tying his shoelaces, waving to his friends in the stadium and glancing sideways at his competitors, or the one who is focused, silent and looking down his lane towards the finishing line?

Paying full attention means that you are aware of being aware. You may also have heard this referred to as being 'in the moment' or being 'present'. Your body is generally relaxed and your breathing is slow. The opposite of this is being on 'automatic pilot' – the state in which most people spend their day-to-day lives and in which bad habits are allowed to repeat themselves.

Abraham Maslow, a noted American psychologist, described full attention as a 'peak experience', because at those times we 'joyfully find ourselves catapulted beyond the confines of the mundane or the ordinary'. I'll have some of that!

But if it is so good, why aren't more of us doing it?

We all understand that our attention spans are challenged each day; our minds are full of chatter and our world is full of distractions, gadgets and stuff to do. We're always being told that we are all busier than ever these days, but sometimes I wonder, are we really? Do we have to be?

I think what has happened is that we have become addicted to distraction, and this has weakened our ability to pay attention. As a result, we are less self-aware and have become less conscious of the impressions we create in others through our behaviour.

Our world caters to this weakness by feeding it: tailor-made smaller-than-bite-sized chunks of information, gadgets designed to tune each other out as well as keep us contactable 24/7.

Let's have a look at some of the things you can do to practise paying attention more fully and to reap the benefits. Attention is like a delicious piece of pie. It is better to savour each mouthful than to sit looking at an empty plate asking yourself, 'Did I just eat all that?' Attention is finite and has a quality that runs from barely there to full and focused. You are, for the most part, in the driver's seat.

case study June: the myth of time management

Over the years, I have observed that people who manage to do more with less effort have certain traits in common – there is nothing random about their seeming effortlessness. How they manage to 'do it all' is not in fact about managing time. If you think about it, you can't actually manage time. Time management is really about managing attention – and tasks.

I was once shopping around for a special birthday gift, when a friend suggested I meet her sister June who, despite having five children under the age of six (including triplets), also ran a small business customising beautiful gift-wrap and stationery. I felt some trepidation about showing up at her house, because I expected that she would be exhausted and stressed out and the house would be chaotic – though I also thought that she might be in need of some grown-up company.

I couldn't have been more wrong (except about the grown-up company). She was calm and focused; the house was chaotic, but just in a 'there's-lots-of-kids-with-toys-around-here' kind of way. June and I sat at her dining table to discuss my gift and look at her work. When I glanced at my watch I was amazed to find that two hours had passed. During that visit not only did I get some beautiful stationery, but I learned something valuable about how June managed to fit in everything that she had to do, and still be so creative and productive.

She told me that she made an appointment with herself every day, usually first thing in the morning, in order to sort out the day's known activities and tasks. She said that at first it was difficult, because quiet moments never seemed to present themselves. Of course these could never be guaranteed, but she did her best to take these moments at least to get the priorities set. She then prioritised in terms of what must happen and what would be nice, but was not essential. Then if possible she arranged what must happen into first, second and third place. For example, she explained that things didn't always go to plan and that it was important to be flexible. There was always an ill babysitter or an unruly child to get in the way of the best intentions. But no matter how many things got undone, there was still a priority. The list might change and the priorities get rearranged, but she would always know in the moment which thing was more important than others. She called it her sanity check.

I was reminded of a technique called 'triage', which originated in World War I. Wounded soldiers were classified into one of three groups: those who could be expected to live without medical care; those who would be likely to die even with care; and those who could survive if they received care. It was this last group who received priority medical attention. June had become head of her own emergency room and was practised at being unsentimental about prioritising her activity.

Then she said the most important thing: 'What makes it all work is that I aim to do just one thing at a time – just one (she said with her finger up) and do it completely and well. Then I move on to the next thing. If I can do that, I'm satisfied.'

By doing one thing at a time in a focused way, most of the time she gets through it all, plus more.

Many people, however, feel that such single-minded focus on one task at a time is impossible, and that multi-tasking is the answer. In my experience, multi-tasking is overrated. It is really just a common and problematical form of distraction from the job in hand.

case study
Harold: misguided multi-tasker

Many people take pride in their perception of their ability to multi-task. They believe they would never be able to cope or 'get through the day' without doing lots of things at once. In most cases, there is a false sense of achievement from performing many tasks simultaneously in a mediocre way, but not doing anything well. Wouldn't these people have achieved more by concentrating on a few tasks and completing those properly, using their full attention for each one?

Don't get me wrong – I don't think having many tasks on the go at the same time is a bad thing as such; it can often be both necessary and productive. It works if, for example, you want to bake a cake and mow the lawn on the same afternoon: you prepare the cake and put it into the oven, then go out to mow the lawn (and of course be sure to finish the lawn before the cake burns!).

I was asked to meet Harold to help him to prepare for a very important and potentially volatile board meeting. He had recently been promoted and when I spoke to him over the phone to schedule our first appointment, he mentioned twice in the space of our brief conversation how overwhelmed he felt with the amount of work the new job would require. In fact, he was so overwhelmed that he needed to do something differently soon or it would start to affect his health. The wall of emails that faced him every morning had become even bigger with his promotion. He had more people reporting to him and more decisions to make. His decisions had more at stake. His solution was to work harder and longer. He believed that the more he could do and the faster he could do it, the better.

Harold rescheduled our appointment twice before we met (because he said he was so overwhelmed), and I noticed that his emails were sent either very late at night or very early in the morning. Was he really at his desk all that time?

When we finally met, I realised Harold was the ultimate multi-tasker. In the hour we were together, he answered his phone three times (very apologetically), responded to the 'beep' on his computer telling him a new email had arrived (many times), received his secretary twice to answer a question, and sent two text messages on his mobile. He also had a radio on quietly in the background.

I noticed too that while Harold was talking with me and dealing with these other tasks at the same time, his body was making a lot of small, quick movements. His foot was tapping rapidly, and he twirled a pen in his hand or fiddled with the button on his jacket. His breathing was shallow and his eyes rarely rested on any one thing for very long. Even our conversation took place in small parts – between other jobs – so that I became one of the multiplicity of tasks he was performing.

I found it difficult to get him to concentrate on the objectives and planning for the meeting, even though I knew his performance there was make-or-break for him. The board needed convincing that he was the right choice for the job and could handle the new responsibilities.

In order to do anything productive, I needed to get him out of his office so we could focus. He was a bit uncomfortable with this suggestion at first – after all, he was 'overwhelmed' with work; couldn't we 'fix it' while he carried on with other things? There was a sense of panic at leaving his office for a quiet meeting room. However, we found one and started talking about his preparations for the board meeting.

It was a perfect opportunity for Harold to pay attention more fully. But could he be convinced that by doing less he would get more done? I discussed my observations with him and, like most multi-taskers, he was quick to defend his output. I assured him that there was no doubt he had the ability to do many things at once. The question was his productivity. As he was taking on more, he needed to be sure he was doing the right things well, not trying to do everything. We discussed some techniques for prioritising, similar to those that June the mother-of-five used, and agreed to some conversations he would have with his boss about workflow and delegation. The intellectual part was easy.

The harder part was now for Harold to learn how to do this on a day-to-day basis. The only way was to replace some of his 'automatic pilot' behaviours with greater awareness and new behaviours.

It is common for multi-taskers to move parts of their body that are not directly involved in the task at hand. If you look closely, you may see two or three other things they are doing at the same time that are not necessary, and that amount to misdirected energy. It may be speaking quickly (and often quite loudly), fidgeting or a tapping of the hands and feet, shallow breathing, nail chewing (notice how nail chewers never remember doing it?) or fiddling with something. There is often tension in the neck, shoulders or back.

Harold did a lot of these things and also tended to stand with his weight on either one foot or the other – rarely equally or in balance. This, combined with his quick-flitting eye contact and fidgeting, created the impression that he was either 'not a deep thinker' or not interested and 'ready to move on to the next thing'. Even though neither may be true, remember my mantra that impressions don't have to be right to matter.

To raise his self-awareness, we worked on how he could do less with his body. We started by having him sit with both feet on the floor, with his hands comfortably in his lap, while we discussed simple subjects in our quiet meeting room. He found this very difficult at first – he kept losing his train of thought. We then added levels of complexity to our discussion so that he needed to pause to collect his thoughts or form an argument. After about ten minutes, he was perspiring and his skin started to flush because of the strain of resisting the extraneous movement.

In our next meeting, we practised in his office environment, surrounded by his office equipment; then we graduated to internal meetings. Initially, Harold was allowed to hold a note pad and make notes as his only other form of activity during conversations or meetings.

After a few short weeks of practising resisting extra movement (combined with a more organised and prioritised workload), Harold reported that his wife had noticed he seemed 'kinder' and 'less stressed' at home. I noticed that he used more eye contact and didn't interrupt as much. We agreed that he would have a new policy of not answering phone calls during scheduled meetings and not texting or emailing during conversations.

Harold's manager and colleagues almost immediately noticed a difference in his level of energy and focus. They were also clearer about their own responsibilities and priorities. A few of them commented that they had enjoyed a more personal relationship with Harold because he had begun to make time to have (albeit brief) conversations with his team about topics other than work.

The report I received a few days after the board meeting was that the board had approved his proposals and felt confident he was 'the man for the job'. In fact, Harold had always been capable of doing the job – he just gave the impression that he was likely to lose control. By paying attention more fully to what it was he was doing to create that impression, replacing the habit of multi-tasking with more deliberate actions, plus prioritising and focusing his efforts, he was able to take on the new job with more confidence and less effort.

I asked him, as I had asked June, to make an appointment with himself every morning – either at home or at work (he said he often did it on the train) that included a sorting of his priority activities and a few minutes of slow breathing and focusing on the tension in his muscles. I asked him to focus on his hands first, then his shoulders, neck and torso. Then his feet, ensuring they were flat on the floor.

The breathing exercises were simple ones: breathing in through his nose for six seconds and out through his mouth for six seconds. Then pausing between breaths and beginning again until he felt more focused and relaxed. Harold now believes that his focus on breathing has made the biggest contribution to his ability to prioritise well. He says that the exercises have given him 'a better perspective on the day's activity'.

case study Jacqui: paying attention to the wrong thing

When I met Jacqui at a family get-together, she spent most of the evening sitting next to me talking about her attempts to pursue her interest in amateur theatre, and her frustration at not getting the parts she was hoping for. She had been auditioning on and off for the last year, with no success. After listening for a while, I asked her why she thought she wasn't being chosen. She said that most of the feedback she was getting was that she was 'too polished'. She was a little confused about this and asked if I would help her.

I'm not an acting coach, but from what I understand about successful actors, a good part of the success lies in achieving authenticity in a role. They draw on their own emotions, memories and experiences to influence the way they play a character. It is less about 'acting' or pretending, and more about whether the audience believes them.

Jacqui and I agreed to meet at my office one Saturday. She brought the script she was to use for her next audition. As she started to read, I could see how she created the impression of being 'too polished'. She just wasn't convincing as the character. It was as though, seconds before she started to read, she flipped a switch. She retreated inside herself, paused, took a breath, moved her eyes into the middle distance and started to speak. Her voice was unnatural and her breathing irregular.

It was as if I wasn't there. She had lost contact with me and from then on I felt completely uninvolved and uninterested. Her performance lacked depth and colour. She might as well have been talking to herself.

This kind of disappearing act is a form of misdirected attention. It means the individual has lost touch with a fundamental fact, which is that the relationship between audience and performer is a two-way street. The audience is made up of individuals, and they will each decide if they have enjoyed it or not. It is not a collective decision – each member of the audience is only ever one person, and a good performer will engage on some level with them all.

Jacqui's problem is common among people who have been coached badly or are just not aware of what they are doing or how to fix it. The 'disappearing act' becomes their communication comfort zone; it can be quite intense and ingrained and therefore uncomfortable to change. Typically, people go from being perfectly natural one second and the next second launching into a 'mode' that takes much more physical and psychological energy to maintain. In Jacqui's case, in order to fix the problem, she needed to engage with her audience rather than just her imagination.

I discussed this with her and asked her to experiment with another approach. She had memorised the text, so for the next reading I wanted her to begin by pausing and making eye contact with me before she spoke, then to maintain full eye contact throughout her speech. This caused her some discomfort and she had to begin again several times. But after about ten minutes, she got the hang of it. She said it made her feel very different. As if she was reading 'for' someone rather than 'to' an audience.

As we practised, her voice sounded more natural, eye contact became easier and her movements grew less mechanical. She said she began to feel the character more as she practised engaging me. I encouraged her to rehearse using full eye contact with her listeners. She was improving so quickly that I was confident she would soon get better feedback and hopefully have some successful auditions!

I got a call from her a week later telling me she had been short-listed for a role in a local theatrical production. She was then chosen for a role (not the one she wanted exactly, but still a big step forward) and was very excited and full of confidence.

A moment of digital distraction

One of the most common challenges to our attention is the seductive nature of communication technology. Some people feel they mustn't be out of the loop, ever, under any circumstances, including holidays, commutes, strolls in the park and naptime – and technology means they don't have to be. There is a price to pay for this. It can affect your career, your health and your relationships. No matter how pervasive or useful the technology becomes, there is still an etiquette that must be obeyed. Draw the line, comrades! Stop the madness. I cannot write a chapter on attention without drawing your attention to the erosion of good manners. Claw them back.

An employee at one of my clients' companies was known as 'text man' by his colleagues, because he had been known to sit in an important meeting and continue to work via text messaging. He struggled with promotion within the company. He thought he was being productive, but others thought he was rude because he had not paid them attention.

Another client told me of a friend of his who didn't answer the phone while they were having dinner. My client was getting edgy and asked, 'Aren't you going to get that?' His friend, surprised to be asked, said, 'No, the phone is there for my convenience.'

Which approach would you choose?

Paying attention more fully to what matters, and keeping in mind that only individuals – not groups – make decisions will help you do more, quickly and with less stress.

Managing physical impressions

Another aspect of paying attention more fully is your awareness of your own body and the impressions you may be creating in other people.

This is important because there is often a big gap between the way we come across to others and the way we intend to. If you are more fully aware of yourself and others, you can more effectively 'read and respond to' your situation.

People form impressions about you before you even open your mouth to speak. In fact, our physical body communicates more than half of the impression we make on others.

One of the most important things to keep in mind about how you create impressions in others (beside the fact that it will happen whether you like it or not), and one of my oft-repeated reminders, is that other people's impressions don't have to be right in order to matter.

We have all experienced situations where we feel we have been treated unfairly or misunderstood. Also, if you ask different people about their impressions of a person or a situation, you are likely to get as many different answers. Your life experience and choices flavour how you create impressions and how you interpret the behaviour of others.

Stephanie Burns is an author and educator who has spent twenty years studying adults, and has come up with something she calls 'Seven Observable Behaviours'. She has identified the main types of behaviours that people observe in forming impressions about us. These seven behaviours are:

- Dress
- Facial expression
- Voice
- Gestures
- Posture
- Movement
- Energy levels

When we observe others, we pick up on a range of signals and then put them together to create a bigger picture. We are capable of unconsciously processing vast amounts of this type of information quickly, and making decisions and judgements without analysing facts or detail. Sounds important enough to pay full attention.

Let me give you a brief top-line of the key points to think about regarding each behaviour.

Dress

This is more about managing distraction than anything else. We all know that your clothes will create a powerful impression immediately if they are inappropriate for the situation. Rule of thumb in terms of what not to wear: if you are in any doubt, don't. There is a lot of expert support and literature on the market to help those who need to learn more about dress.

Remember that the impact clothing has on your and others' ability to pay full attention is huge. If what you are wearing is uncomfortable, hot and scratchy or even not warm enough, if you are over- or underdressed, something has torn or is falling off or too tight or ill fitting, you know how hard it is to focus. People looking at you feel the same. Too much exposed flesh in the wrong place, a vibrant colour, a stain. Dinner party stories are made of these incidents!

Facial expression

I find that the most problematical issue with facial expression is when someone's face does not match the emotion they are intending to communicate. This happens often in business, where people have learned to 'mask' their feelings. This takes the form of either too much expression or not enough. It confuses or dazzles other people, and the person concerned gets labelled as 'hard to read'. A badge of honour for some, but a source of frustration for others. If your facial expressions are considered 'hard to read', think about listening more actively. In Chapter Six I refer to active acknowledgement giving the other person a clue about what you are thinking, or at least that you are listening.

Voice

'Our voices are the windows to our souls,' said a famous voice coach, but unless you are a professional actor or singer you probably don't think much about your voice and how you use it. The voice is a reflection of your state of mind and your physical condition. The tone and resonance give clues to levels of tension, emotion and even authenticity.

The two most common problems are tension in the neck and tongue, often caused by nervousness, which can create a higher pitch to the voice. The other is pushing the voice down or lower – also often caused by nerves, which can make it sound monotonous. Breathing is important. If you are not breathing properly, you are creating something other than your own, natural voice. Again, there is a lot of literature and expert help out there for learning voice control and breathing techniques. But your main focus should be to relax your shoulders and find your rhythm by breathing slowly, from your diaphragm.

Gesture

Gesturing is a natural and necessary part of communicating. Hands act as our punctuation marks and add emphasis and colour to what we are saying or doing. The most important thing to remember about gesturing is to know when not to do it – in other words, when to rest your hands. Get comfortable and aware of what you are doing with your hands when you are not using them. Actually practise resting your hands during conversation, and you will find you use them more naturally when you need to.

Posture and movement

I have put these together because they are closely linked. Bad posture is very common. We develop it over the years from a lack of awareness about our bodies, lack of exercise, the wrong exercise, bad chairs, poor diet or health, lack of self confidence or just too much travel or tiredness. For me, in my work with clients, I find posture and movement the 'low-hanging fruit' for increased awareness, and therefore very useful elements to work on. Our bodies are a sculptural representation of how we feel and think.

The most significant change you can bring about for yourself is to become more aware of, and participate with fuller attention in, the type of activity that allows you to consciously align and control your body more often. This means becoming more aware of how you stand, sit, rest, lift, balance, move, exercise and breathe in your day-to-day life. I have found the principles of yoga, tai chi and the Alexander technique particularly helpful and practical.

Energy levels

This is not about what you say, but how you feel or make others feel. It is linked to how badly you want to do what you are doing, how much you care or don't care about something, and to your level of involvement. Of course your health can also affect your energy levels. Energy levels are about more than just how much you move around, the loudness of your voice, or how you work a room.

Being described as either 'lazy' or 'charismatic' can often be a clue as to how others are interpreting your energy levels. What I have found most interesting about other people's impressions of energy is that they are often associated with how well you may have connected – or not – with them. In particular, how interested they feel you are in them. I have heard the laziest people described as charismatic, because they perfected the knack of putting their full attention on someone during a conversation. Dale Carnegie's advice on winning friends and influencing people is still as relevant as ever! Be aware, there is a lot of mileage to be gained by simply putting your attention on others.

So there are as many ways to practise paying full attention as there are demands on it. In order to gain the rewards available to you, I advise you to invest the time and effort. There are benefits to you, your relationships, health, well-being and career. When you start paying more attention you will get more attention in return. You will get more done in your day and have a richer experience of the world around you.

chapter **eight**

knowing when not to

Think for a moment about situations where you were glad or relieved that you had chosen not to act. You chose not to say something you would have regretted during a tense or emotional discussion, or not to give an opinion during a meeting at work, or not to tell that joke at a party or poke fun at something or someone, or not to take action on a decision or a proposal, or not to take that job or pursue that opportunity. And in retrospect you were grateful.

What is it that compels us to know when not to? Is it fate or a universal force that chooses to protect us from harm? Is it just experience and wisdom that we have gained over years of learning and making mistakes? If I could answer that, I think I would corner the market on having a hassle-free life!

There was some recent research conducted to determine what it is that makes a person wise. Believe it or not, there are people called 'wisdom researchers' who have been studying the subject for years. One of them, Stephen Hall, explained some of the qualities of wisdom, which included 'a clear-eyed view of human nature, emotional resiliency and the ability to cope in the face of adversity, an openness to possibilities, forgiveness, humility, a knack for learning from lifetime experiences... Emotion is central to wisdom, yet detachment is essential.' He added, 'Action is important, but so is judicious inaction' – in other words, knowing when not to. The studies also state that while wisdom is generally found in those with more life experience, it is not limited to older people. Often wisdom can come from adversity or even experiences from your early childhood that have shaped your outlook on life.

Researchers have devoted many years to developing metrics for measuring wisdom, and one thing is certain: people who score low on the wisdom scale tend to have a 'preoccupation with self'.

In a world that rewards action and 'doing', giving a considered or appropriate response is not something we do naturally or easily. As a consequence, getting it right does not come naturally.

I believe we are just out of practice. I think one can practise wise behaviours and, in doing so, become wiser.

Don't be fooled, practising wise behaviour is not easy. How often have you felt that inappropriate words 'just came out of my mouth' or confessed afterwards that 'I didn't realise what I was doing'? This is common, owing to a general lack of awareness about how we affect others.

This is what the wisdom researchers I mentioned earlier refer to as 'preoccupation with self'. So practising wise behaviours has a double benefit. It will help you understand how your behaviour affects others (thus be wiser) and to make better, more informed, responses (thus be wiser).

This chapter will focus on my experience of working with clients in situations where they needed to practise knowing when not to, and when changing their communication habits was their key to getting it right more often.

I will focus on three of the most common unwise communication behaviours my clients have asked me to help them with:

- knowing when not to say something
- knowing when not to get involved in a relationship – business or personal
- knowing when not to dig your heels in

Knowing when not to say something

Most of us throw our common sense out of the window when we are faced with an emotionally charged situation. We all have different ways of dealing with emotion and when the tension rises, some of us get ultra cool and silent, while others get louder and more boisterous. Either response is appropriate – when it is appropriate. Herein lies the problem.

I have had a number of clients over the years who limited their career options because of how they mismanaged responses. The most common type of problem I was asked to deal with in the workplace was how people react to their emotional tension. Some people have a habit of lashing out in anger at a co-worker, embarrassing someone in a meeting by arguing with them or putting them down in front of others. It isn't serious enough to get themselves fired, but is just enough to keep them from being promoted or becoming a productive member of their team.

This also happens in our personal lives. Certain people just know exactly how to upset us. Sometimes it is very difficult to know how to avoid the same old thing. They press the button, you respond! Sound familiar?

I know, you can hear your conscience saying, 'I told you so – you never listen to me.' But there are a few common-sense guidelines to consider before responding in this way:

■ It is important to think about the consequences of an argument or the action. Is it worth it?
■ Don't fight over or get involved with something that's none of your business, or that you can't do anything about.
■ If you are angry, what is it really about? Identify what is behind your anger before you rush in and address the wrong, superficial issue.

- Make sure that what you say or do is going to solve something.
- Don't argue or say something just because you 'feel you've been challenged' or get involved 'because you have been asked'.
- Ask yourself, 'Is it really a big deal?' Chances are that it's not.
- Realise that you don't always have to have the last word, and often it takes a better person to simply let a conflict go.
- Ask yourself, 'Am I really right? Does it matter if I'm right? Is there really a "right or wrong" for this issue?'
- Is this an issue you'll remember in five years? In one year or six months, even? If not, don't take it on.

One of my dear friends, Corina, works from home and told me about a technique she uses to keep her work pressures from getting in the way of a harmonious family life. Anyone who has ever worked at home knows how difficult it can be to draw the line between where work finishes and home begins. Often conflicts occur in otherwise loving or friendly relationships, not because there is genuine friction between two people, but because it just wasn't the right time to discuss something.

The technique Corina uses is called HALT. Essentially, it means being prepared to not say or do anything for a moment if you're:

- hungry
- angry
- lonely (or hurt)
- tired (or under time pressure)

If you are any of these, halt. Eat the meal you skipped, calm down if you're angry, don't hide away if you're lonely or hurt, take a break if you are overworked. Obviously, if you're in two or more of these states you really need to halt! HALT is a useful tool because so often immediate, physical, knee-jerk responses result in us saying or doing something we wish we hadn't.

It may mean keeping out of an escalating conflict. Holding your tongue instead of saying something you may regret. Not answering an emotionally loaded question on the spot. Waiting to make an important decision. Not saying or doing anything until you take time to figure out your feelings. Practise saying, 'I'll get back to you on that.' Or, 'Let me think about it first.'

Corina told me about a common occurrence. When she is working late on a project – usually because she has a tight deadline – her spouse often pops his head around the door to ask when she will be finished. She has missed dinner and is hungry, tired and mildly annoyed at the way he puts pressure on her. If she isn't careful she may say something that will hurt his feelings or make the situation worse. So she halts and pauses, allowing herself time to sort out her feelings and thoughts and say something like, 'I'm progressing pretty well right now and I'm not sure how much longer I will be. I will let you know as I get closer to my finish time.'

The key is to be consistent and stick to what you have said you will do. In other words, don't move the goalposts or create a situation where you might have to. Don't exaggerate or fudge the response. Keep it neutral.

In these times of hyper-awareness regarding politically correct language, I worry that the playfulness of good old-fashioned spontaneity could die a death. Sometimes, speaking without thinking does no (real) harm at all. My friend Jill, who is a very good golfer, told me of an occasion she was in a sports shop comparing different kinds of golf balls – she was unhappy with the women's type she had been using. After browsing for several minutes, she was approached by a young shop assistant who asked if he could help. Without thinking, she said, 'I think

I like playing with men's balls.' She then realised what she'd said, blushed, and they both laughed.

If you are lucky, when these humorous faux pas happen you can retell the story with a smile on your face.

However, when unthinking comments are not one-offs, but a continual stream, they can erode credibility and damage relationships.

 case study Steve: saying the wrong thing at the right time

I heard about Steve through a mutual friend who was concerned that his friends were beginning to avoid him, and that he was suffering professionally because of a particular bad habit. He had a tendency to say the wrong thing at the right time, or the right thing at the wrong time. His comments were often witty, but they were also insensitive, and undermined what other people had said. Steve's former boss and mentor had recently retired, but before he left the company he had advised Steve that this 'wisecracking' behaviour was something he would have to change if he was to progress further in the firm.

A few weeks later, Steve and I were introduced at a dinner party and before the end of the evening I could see what my friend was talking about. In addition to the wisecracks, Steve would also occasionally say something that would end a subject abruptly, because no one knew how to respond. Some of the guests even chose to take their coffee into another room to continue their conversations, but Steve didn't seem to pick up on any signals, subtle or not, from other people. If this was happening at work, I could see the cause for concern. Steve was a challenging presence, and his behaviour was chipping away at important relationships with his peers and his new boss.

Steve and I met soon afterwards to discuss how I could help.

I think we all know someone like Steve, who seems to have a knack for embarrassing or undermining others in this way. In my experience, these people are in one of two camps: they either know they do it and enjoy the attention; or they are nervous and awkward, ignorant of the effect their endless comments are having on others. Steve was in the second camp. He wasn't mean or nasty, just plain annoying and best avoided.

I am not interested in the reasons why someone behaves the way they do, only in what to do when they are ready to change their behaviour.

Steve and I discussed his problem for a while, and I asked him to experiment with a few new behaviours in his meetings the following week at work.

First, we began with the obvious, which was his understanding of the emotional impact of his comments on others and his underlying intention. He agreed it was not productive and that nothing would change for the better if he kept on doing it.

Next, I asked him to blend more questions – rather than statements or observations – into his conversations and meetings. To ensure that they were not just versions of his statements, we crafted some relevant questions around the topics and the people involved in his upcoming meetings, and rehearsed them.

To help him resist the impulse to blurt out a statement, I wanted him to be more aware of the physical posture he adopted while he was listening to others. I also wanted him to see how this posture – leaning slightly forwards – actually facilitated his tendency to blurt out a comment when any opportunity arose.

Steve was evidently uncomfortable with pauses or lulls in conversation. When someone else was speaking, he would appear alert, his posture upright, leaning slightly forwards. His eye contact would move from the person speaking to others round the table, watching their responses. When he made his comments, he either looked around the room for the response, or completely withdrew. To an observer, it felt as though he was poised for entering and leaving conversations abruptly. This had an unsettling effect on everyone else in the room, as they were unable to gauge his degree of involvement at any one time.

I asked that, along with asking more questions, he sit slightly back in his chair – his spine relaxed, but comfortably upright – creating the feeling that he was still involved in the conversation but not leaning so far forwards that he dominated it. I asked him either to rest his hands lightly in his lap or place them gently on the table. This was an extreme change for him and at first he struggled to remember the questions when we practised the more relaxed physical postures. He was accustomed to sitting tensely upright – as he said, 'almost like I was at the starting line'.

After two weeks, some more practice, and some interim phone calls, we got together again to discuss how he was progressing. He said he found the hardest task was to resist the urge to say something he thought was funny or memorable, but that entering a meeting more prepared for the topic and knowing more about the individuals in the room made it easier for him to ask questions. He felt more relaxed and learned more from the meetings. The last I heard, his peers had voted Steve to be their employee works council (union) representative. He was rightly very proud of this.

He told me he was also practising at home and with friends. As a single man, applying this technique had improved his success with meeting new women! He realised that on dates he used to try too hard to be witty and the centre of attention. Consequently, he talked too much too soon and overwhelmed rather than charmed. An additional benefit of knowing when not to say something!

Knowing when not to get involved with someone

This is not a chapter about how to avoid bad romantic relationships. It may, however, help you recognise when someone may not be worth getting involved with. Like you, I have sat with many a friend over a sad or anxious cup of coffee discussing the latest break-up or problem person.

When it comes to making decisions about getting into relationships – business or personal – we are all human: we make mistakes when 'reading' others and feel as if 'we should have seen it coming'. Life is a constant effort to align different versions of the truth – your version and someone else's. The closer these versions get, the more likely we are to have a good or peaceful relationship. Conversely, when we get it wrong, people enter our lives who do not add anything – or worse, drain us. The key is to avoid repeating the same mistakes, or to notice when you have made one and get out of it quickly.

First things first – you and your version of the truth.

Aside from your initial gut feeling about other people usually being right, there are two fundamental principles you need to know about yourself before you can know when not to get involved with someone.

The first is that you don't deserve to have bad or troublesome people in your life. Really! This belief means you set personal boundaries that allow you to protect and take care of yourself. You effectively draw a line in the sand past which you will not walk. It means you are not prepared to accept certain kinds of behaviour.

The second principle is that you must be prepared not to blame others for the way you feel – or to judge them. 'You hurt me, you embarrassed me, you deceived me', and because of that 'you are weird or mean, or stupid'. It's not about them, it's about their effect on you, and you need to concentrate on this being your priority.

By not blaming or judging, you can be more objective and stay free of value judgements, something that may involve you unnecessarily. Instead, try standing back and thinking, 'That person seems fearful or full of anger and it would be better if I was not involved with them.' If you think about it, all you can really do is observe them. The rest is guesswork.

There are sometimes other, darker forces at work that guide us to repeating bad habits, but we won't be able to deal with them here – save them for your analyst! But aside from these, and even without the benefit of perfect foresight, setting boundaries can help you retain some control when embarking on new relationships, and so provide an easier escape hatch should you decide you want out.

You have to set the boundaries in the knowledge that other people may not be willing or able to change their behaviour – and be prepared to take whatever action you need to if that proves to be the case. That action may be as dramatic as cutting someone out of your life completely. Sometimes we are afraid to set boundaries because it means hurting someone, making others angry or losing a relationship. But remember that it's worth standing up for yourself, even if people don't like it or may go away.

Now that you have agreed to set boundaries because it is good for you and those around you, and you have taken responsibility for your feelings by not judging or blaming – what does it look like when you put it into practice?

case study **Nigel: used and abused**

My friend Nigel is one of those wonderful people who somehow always ends up with the wrong people around him professionally and personally. The theme running through each conflict is people taking advantage of his good nature and generosity with his time, attention and money. The problem is that it keeps happening. Over one particular cup of coffee, I decided to talk to him about setting some personal boundaries. We practised some conversations he needed to have with his latest partner, who was always turning up late or cancelling arrangements at the last minute.

'Boundary language' has three parts:

- 'when....'
- 'I feel...'
- 'I want...'

'When... (observing a behaviour) you make a dinner reservation with me and don't show up, and give me a last minute excuse, I feel... (owning your feelings, communicating them directly) angry, hurt, discounted. I want... (be clear and reasonable) you to start showing up on time.'

If the person does not change their behaviour, try round two of boundary language:

- 'if you...'
- 'I will...'
- 'if you continue this behaviour...'

'If you.... (describe the behaviour you find unacceptable) keep making plans and not showing up, I will.... (describe the action you will take to protect the boundary) consider that it means you do not value my friendship. If you continue this behaviour… (say what steps you'll take to protect the boundary you set) I will not do anything for you again.'

This approach can work in other contexts, too. The other issue Nigel had with his partner, apart from her casual disregard for his time, was her inability to communicate directly when she was upset. So we use boundary language again:

'When… I ask you what is wrong and you say "nothing" and then start slamming doors and generally seem to be quietly raging about something, I feel…. angry, frustrated and irritated, as if you are unwilling to communicate with me and I am supposed to read your mind. I want… you to communicate with me and help me understand if I have done something that upsets you.'

And if it continues….

'If you… are bothered by something and you will not tell me what it is, I will… confront you about your behaviour, tell you how I feel and insist we talk to a counsellor together. If you keep repeating this behaviour… I will start considering my options, including leaving this relationship.'

The only catch here is that you have to be realistic about the consequences and be sure they are something you want and are prepared to carry through. It is not enough just to set the boundaries, you have to be willing to protect them. Nigel had a habit of allowing his boundaries to be ignored and not forcing the other person to feel the consequences of breaching them. He has told me he does now appreciate the need to set boundaries, and he practises this earlier in his relationships. Yes, he still moves in and out of relationships often, but now at least he feels he has more control and feels the relationships are richer, less stressful and, in his words, more 'grown-up'.

It is near to impossible to have a relationship with someone who can't set boundaries or communicate directly and honestly. Here are a few choice sentences that may get you thinking about your own situation if you need to – things that you might say to someone who steps over the line:

- 'I need to communicate if we have a misunderstanding.'
- 'I won't accept your condescending jokes or your criticism.'
- 'I won't be disrespected – if you won't respect me, stay away.'
- 'If we are going to work together I need honesty, respect and fairness.'
- 'Don't vent your anger on me – I won't have it.'
- 'I want openness in a relationship – your withholding is making our relationship unsatisfying for me.'

There is an unsavoury irony to all this. People who attract problem people are usually those who have a desire to be liked and/or a generous and trusting nature. I can't deal with the forces that may drive this behaviour – but believe me when I say that by replacing the behaviour we can go a long way towards making it less of a problem.

 case study Monica:
reading the tell-tale signs

Another aspect of knowing when not to get involved with someone is when that person's version of the truth is a lie. Okay, we all sometimes massage the facts to a certain extent, but even so it is good to be able to spot the clues.

Monica runs a recruitment agency that specialises in domestic staff. It is a very competitive business and hers had started to grow very quickly. She asked if I would come in and have a look at how she was recruiting people, and give her some ideas about how to improve her interviewing process. Could she get better at knowing when not to hire someone? In particular, could she more easily read if they were telling the whole truth about themselves, regardless of references or other checking mechanisms?

Over a period of a couple of days I sat through about 25 of their 'typical' interviews. Details and references checked, then a half-hour one-to-one conversation. One of the most glaring improvements I noticed they could make was to reduce the number of closed questions they asked (see page 120). Too many required only yes/no answers rather than asking for an opinion or an explanation. There weren't enough ways to explore the applicants' feelings or thoughts about any situation deeply enough. Without doing this, they could never get closer to 'reading' the interviewee.

So Monica and I discussed introducing more open questions that could be followed with, 'Tell me more about that' or, 'Why do you feel that way?' and, 'How did you do that?'

I then ran a short workshop on the body language generally associated with deviating from the truth. Apart from the skilled sociopaths who can fool lie detector tests, I believe that most people want to do the right thing, and so there is a natural physical tension that occurs in people who are lying – there is a subtle mismatch between the words we speak and the message our body conveys. Some things to look out for are:

■ A higher pitched voice, hesitation, choosing wrong words or bad sentence structure, unusual eye contact, pupil dilation, blinking or rubbing their eyes often.
■ Inappropriate laughter – too much or too loud.
■ Their bodies may be rigid. Because they are trying to over-control their body, you may see conflicting signals – shrug and

grimace, fidgeting hands and feet, smiling mouth but not the eyes, oversized gestures compared to what they are saying, or very small movements drawn into the body.

■ Sighing inappropriately or shallow breathing.

■ They might put physical barriers between you – a briefcase or purse, a table, folded arms, books or papers.

■ Overcompensating by looking too relaxed, nonchalant, going into too much detail, using too much eye contact.

■ Rambling on about things that are irrelevant or inconsequential.

■ Getting defensive or using humour or sarcasm in an attempt to avoid a subject.

■ A statement with a contraction ('didn't' rather than 'did not') is more likely to be truthful, as Bill Clinton so neatly demonstrated with his, 'I did not have relations with that woman' rather than, 'I didn't have relations with that woman.'

■ They may repeat back your exact words to answer a question: 'Did you take my socks?' Answer: 'No, I did not take your socks.'

■ When asked to describe a situation where they were unsuccessful, they will not usually talk about the negative aspects, the thing that went wrong. They also may blame others.

Over the next round of interviews, Monica and her team combined these insights with the new questioning techniques. They reported back that they found the interviews more interesting and dynamic, and learned more about the applicants, thereby helping them make better 'matches' with clients. Importantly, they learned which topics to explore further and which pieces of the 'truth' to double check. A good question or pause at the right time can reveal a lot.

At the end of three months, turnover (people who failed to stay on after the initial period they were hired for) had gone down by 20 per cent. A good result for the agency, given that quality people were important for its reputation as well as for managing the cost of firing and hiring. And, in this context, of course, it was not always about recognising if someone was lying, but about finding the right 'fit' for the job as well.

Using these tell-tale signs is not an exact art. 'Reading' is about noticing more than just one of these signals (usually two or three at the same time), and you need to factor in the context of what the person is saying before making a judgement about them. It is also good to have a second opinion, in case you are overzealous in seizing on what might be innocent tics. Just because someone fidgets or perspires or stutters it doesn't mean they are dishonest. Sometimes crossing your arms is just comfortable, that's it!

Understanding yourself, accepting responsibility for your feelings and setting boundaries for others goes a long way towards knowing when not to get involved with someone. But that is only part of the answer. If you can improve your powers of observation you can read signals others send us about their level of intention or sincerity. The closer you get your version of the truth to match theirs, the better off you will be!

Knowing when not to dig your heels in

Always needing to be right and in control has got to be one of the most tedious personality traits on the planet. My apologies to those of you who throughout your life have put time and effort into perfecting the art – I don't mean to upset you.

Well, maybe I do, actually.

So what does this have to do with knowing when not to dig your heels in? 'Digging your heels in' means refusing to yield or compromise. It is important to know when not to hold your ground, be stubborn, be right or obstinate, because it puts you and others into a 'corner'. This is a major obstacle to developing relationships with others.

One of the most common types of challenges I am asked to become involved with is the person who believes 'it's my way or the highway'. In other words, they know best, they are right, and they are not always very nice about it. This is a problem not only because of the difficulties it creates when working in a team, but also because the truth is that no one person has all the answers. Unique as each one of us is, there is always someone out there who could do our job as well or better.

 case study **Molly: no trust, no staff**

I met Molly a few months after she had been elected leader of over two hundred volunteer staff at a major charity. This is a role that demands long hours and the goodwill of many people who work for no pay. It also requires her to be very organised – a skill which Molly has in abundance. But after I had spent some time with her, I realised that there was one aspect of her style that was going to give her trouble. Molly believed she had to control everything: from ordering stationery and the minutiae of the scheduling of daily tasks of the volunteer staff, to whether a handmade invitation had red or yellow bordering. Not only did she want to control every aspect of her team's work, but she wasn't open to other people's ideas. This was compounded by asking for input from her team, but hardly ever using it.

The alarm bells went off when the number of volunteer staff started to shrink – for the first time in the charity's history. Those who left said it was because of Molly's high-handed approach to managing them. Those who remained said that much of the fun had gone out of their work. Time to do something.

The problem with people who try to over-control is that they are often convinced that if they didn't behave this way, the world around them would fall apart. They also believe that they are the only ones who can do the job. Molly needed to understand that the charity had been there before she arrived and would be there after she left. The contribution of the sum of the individuals who worked there was more important than any one person's input.

Philosophically, Molly had to get her head around her place in the world. She also had to learn to trust herself and others. Physically, she needed to try some new behaviours that might help her salvage her situation. Over-controlling is exhausting on a body. It is one part intellectual and seven parts emotional!

When Molly was working, she had many things happening at the same time. Because she wanted to check everything or approve everything, there were a lot of items 'waitlisted', or waiting to be seen. This meant she had very long days – her schedule was packed with appointments, proposals were waiting to be read late into the night, work conversations took place at weekends and odd hours. She didn't delegate minor tasks, so she spent too much time on things that could be handled by someone else.

She was looking tired and carrying tension in her shoulders and lower back. She also had another physical trait common among over-controllers. I call it 'punctuation'. It means that she used her body and speech in a way that was almost like punctuation. When there was an issue on which she would not budge, she subtly overemphasised key words or the last letter in a word at the end of her sentences. Her gestures became more definite – particularly the 'chopping' gesture (like chopping something on a board). If she felt someone was disagreeing with her, she used all this, and leaned in to the person she was about to speak to, as if to 'underline' her conviction. She did this equally with a smile or a frown on her face.

Not surprisingly, Molly made far more statements than she asked questions. The effect was that she 'told' others what she wanted and she physically 'punctuated' her commands. This did not create the feeling that compromise was possible, or invited.

To bring about the biggest changes, two communication behaviours had to be introduced. Molly needed to:

1 Neutralise her physical punctuation. This meant taking the vocal and physical stress off the key ideas she wanted to push through. This was difficult for her. She said that communicating her idea without this physical behaviour was like 'letting the dog run without a leash'.

2 Ask more genuinely open questions. Molly had the habit of asking leading questions that would imply the answer she wanted, so that, 'Do you think the timing is right on this – particularly in light of the amazing research that was done?' could become, 'How do you feel about the timing?' or, 'Does anyone have a comment on timing?' Or, instead of, 'I really like this. Does anyone have any compelling reason why it shouldn't happen?' she could say, 'I am interested in your views on this idea.' After gathering the views she would then ask, 'What would block this idea from happening?' or, 'Can anyone think of a reason why we shouldn't do it?'

Aside from her communication behaviours, Molly's other major obstacle was her reluctance and inability to delegate. This element of her controlling nature was the major source of both dissatisfaction among her staff and stress and exhaustion for Molly herself. It was crucial that Molly should understand and believe that most people did want to assume responsibility, and that delegating was the right option for her to make. She needed to trust people to get on with the job and to not look over their shoulder, or check up on them. (By this time she was squirming in her chair.)

We outlined some guidelines for Molly to use when handing work over to volunteer staff:

1 Delegate to the right person – this person is not always the strongest or best or most available. In other words, if the best person for the job is already very busy, or the most available person is does not have the requisite skills for that particular job, move down the list.

2 Delegate the objective, not the procedure. State the desired results, not a step-by-step explanation of how to do it.

3 When you have finished giving instructions, ask, 'What else do you need to get started?'

4 Ask now and then, simply, 'How is it going with the project?'

5 Give praise and feedback at the end of the project – and maybe even more responsibility.

We spent a couple of weeks practising how Molly would create a more collaborative style of working, and what she would have to do differently in physical terms. We began by prioritising her tasks and sorting out her specific role objectives and responsibilities. Her biggest task, however, was to win back the hearts and minds of her volunteer staff.

After a few months, Molly and I met for dinner. She told me that things were going well at the charity and her volunteer numbers were higher than they had ever been. Many of the original volunteers had returned once the news had spread that she was changing her approach. She had won their support and was enjoying working with a more creative and motivated staff.

Molly also said that her husband had commented on how much more relaxed she seemed, and that he was enjoying some new-found attention at the weekends since she had cleared her schedule.

Good for Molly. She took responsibility for her behaviour, acknowledged that it wasn't working and took another course of action that paid off immediately.

Many people get themselves into difficult situations because they can't acknowledge they are wrong. They are not comfortable with apologising, and this inability or reluctance to say sorry leaves them with a lot of regret or damaged relationships.

I remember being called by my friend Kelly after her family holiday. She sounded distressed and when I asked her about it she told me that she had misbehaved terribly over a three-day stay with her mother, and needed to pluck up the courage to apologise. I didn't probe for too many details except to ask why she felt she needed to apologise. I know she has had a very stressful relationship with her mother over the years.

It was all very complex now, but this time Kelly had had too much to drink, had criticised the cooking in front of everyone and flirted openly with her sister's boyfriend. It couldn't be better if it was a movie. I'm glad she couldn't see me smiling. An apology seemed a galaxy away in her mind.

The wonderful part of an apology is its power. It can mend a broken heart, soothe wounded pride or heal a fractured relationship. Particularly if you are in the wrong, or if you just want to start somewhere, like Kelly, there are some important steps to take. According to psychologists, there are three aspects to a successful apology. These are: being willing to accept responsibility for your actions ('Mum, I was out of line and I am sorry'), regretting what you did ('I feel terrible about it') and being willing to take some action to remedy it ('I'll never do that again. I will apologise directly to everyone for my behaviour').

Let's say that you are in a situation where you and another person are both to blame. You may have had a heated argument at work about a matter that the next day seems trivial. One of you needs to initiate an apology. Doing so sets the scene for the other person to apologise too. The next day at the coffee machine you say, 'I think we owe each other an apology. I'd like to start by saying I'm sorry for yesterday's misunderstanding.' The only catch is that you have to be ready to do it without any resentment or caveats.

It is possible that the other person doesn't agree, is still upset and is not willing to accept your apology. That's okay – you have done your bit and you need to accept that they may not come round to your point of view. You can at least feel better because you have admitted the mistake and are showing you empathise with how your actions may have affected someone else. And however complex or long-running an argument or problem might be, a genuine apology, as a gesture of goodwill, is a good start. In Kelly's case, her apology was warmly received, her behaviour was forgiven and there was every sign it could mark the beginnings of an improvement in long-term mother-daughter relations.

Apologies are a little like going swimming in cold water. If you do it a little at a time it can be painful. You have to go in full body. Once you are in, the water's fine!

There are times when you should not apologise. That is, when you don't feel you are in the wrong. Be sure you are responsible for something before you own it!

So, knowing when not to is not after all very mysterious. Unless you find yourself in a cycle of repeating things you regret – which is a different matter – you can go quite a long way simply by knowing how to extricate yourself from the inevitable slip-up.

Success in this is partly to do with having the courage to try something new, and partly to do with already having had the experience to know better. Still, we make mistakes. I think on the road to wisdom you can behave wisely.

chapter **nine**

getting comfortable
with silence

Are you uncomfortable with even brief moments of silence? Do you feel the need to turn the TV or the radio on – not to watch, but to have the background noise? I know several people who can't sleep unless the TV or radio is on. Do you feel compelled to pick up a book or just do something? What would happen if you decided just to sit silently for a few moments?

In terms of walking around your boulders completely, becoming comfortable with silence will play a large part in your success, and will strengthen your resolve to continue. Silence is addictive – once you get a taste for what it can do, you will be hooked. It is where you will source your strength to do what you need to do.

Think about these moments as space between thoughts. For most of us there is no such thing.

Our noisy external world doesn't make it easy for us. During a delay in an airport lounge years ago, I met a noise pollution researcher. His greatest concern was that we were raising a whole generation of young people who believed the world was naturally a loud place. 'Stupid man-made noises', he called them. Other people's iPods, alarms (now your car beeps when you lock and unlock it), car radios, loud conversations on mobile phones, air traffic, engines, and the list goes on.

You can recognise if you need to become more comfortable with silence when you:

- do most of the talking
- jump in with advice before an issue is clarified
- use a break or silence in conversation to create distraction, by changing the subject
- interrupt by talking over someone else

- think about your response before someone has finished talking
- respond quickly with little or no thought
- attempt to be clever, charming, competent, impressive
- talk in circles with nothing new emerging

The truth is that we need silence, both personally and professionally. We need to make the moments of space available to ourselves. So let's first look at some of the most common ways we show discomfort with silence, and then some ways you can create space between thoughts.

Discomfort with silence

One of the most common ways of showing discomfort with silence is to talk over it and fill in the blanks with words. We are not taught to like silence. Many of my clients over the years have struggled with how to manage silence in negotiations, conversations, presentations and meetings. There is a general fear of a silent room – 'What if nobody says anything?' or, 'The silence seemed to go on forever' even when it was really just seconds. We believe that our answers have to be quick and ready; we need explanations, and to demonstrate action, movement and confidence. The result is that we talk at each other, not with each other. We are so busy playing the role of 'expert', or being dynamic and clever, that we fill up the airspace as if we are in transmit mode. As a result, we often miss what may really be going on. We are lost in transmission!

case study Paul: stuck in transmit mode

I met Paul after he had had a very unsuccessful series of meetings with a group of board members in his company, who then decided that he was not going to receive the promotion he had hoped to get. Two years previously, he had been identified as a candidate who would be most likely to succeed the chief executive, and the negative outcome of this meeting was a big let-down. Paul hadn't seen it coming. He was disappointed and confused.

After about 30 minutes with him, I could identify the core of the problem. Paul talked too much. He filled every possible space with sound. He spoke in a monotone voice, quickly paced, with the words strung together without a break. He ignored my attempts to interrupt, and when I did get through (once), he didn't listen to what I had said, and kept on with his train of thought. At times he would be lively and animated as if to engage me, but kept the words strung tightly together so that I had no opportunity to contribute to the conversation. My attention was flagging and I was starting to get aggravated. I tried to interject with questions and comments, but he talked over me. His interruptions often took the form of finishing my sentences or thoughts, then adding some amusing aside or an example from his own experience. These were almost always relevant and interesting, but they were nonetheless interruptions.

I felt the best approach was to be very direct with him. (Maybe the only way to cut through his talk!) So in our next meeting, I started our conversation by outlining my observations. I told him that the last time we met I had felt he talked non-stop and I couldn't get a word in. When I had managed to say something, he hadn't listened, but had kept on talking. I also told him I received feedback from the board meetings, and that the members were left with the impression that he had spent the whole time 'talking at them', rather than engaging them in a dialogue. This led them to believe that Paul would not be a good listener.

While I was explaining this to him, I noticed that he was trying to interrupt me. I pointed this out to him also. He jumped in to change the subject. I pointed this out to him also.

He then sat quietly and asked, 'So what do I do?'

I suggested that we should allow for some silences as we talked, so we could sit and experience what it felt like. During our conversation, he caught himself breaking the silence, and corrected himself as we went along. He acknowledged that he had been told before by friends and colleagues that he talked too much, but never took it very seriously. He admitted that he was concerned that he wouldn't be as interesting or dynamic if he spoke less.

Practising not talking is a relevant exercise for people who talk too much, but Paul had to practise silence in other parts of his life as well as in his speech. In other words, it wasn't as simple as me asking him to 'just stop talking'. He needed to create situations where he could be alone. This isn't easy for a lot of people, and in our busy world is often seen as self-indulgent. Silence can mean choosing not to speak for a while, but it also means periodically withdrawing from such activities as watching television, listening to the radio, or reading a book.

I recommended that Paul started with a journal exercise. He was to write about an issue that interested him for an uninterrupted fifteen minutes per day. This would allow him to express himself in silence.

Another action involved adding some new vocabulary to his conversations. Things such as, 'I'd like a moment to reflect on what you've said' or, 'This is a really important topic. Let's slow it down a little so we can both absorb what we are saying.' Or that old favourite, 'Tell me more about that.' We also changed the way he 'set up' his meetings and conversations. Instead of starting off a conversation with a statement, he would practise putting the focus on his conversation partner with a type of question that would be more likely to open up the other person and keep the conversation going two-way. I have covered these types of questions in Chapter Five.

I also asked him to pause quietly for one or two breaths before responding or making statements. This sounds mechanical, but it gave him a useful and challenging guideline. He told me that after two weeks of practising this breathing technique, he found that the tone and even the subject took on a new dimension. Even in these short seconds of pause, he noticed that the other person often jumped in and rescued the silence, said something else or clarified, giving him interesting insight. Other people spent more time talking, and there was more of a balanced sharing of airwaves.

These few techniques were difficult for him at first. But after three weeks, he had a respectable groundswell of people commenting that he seemed 'much more relaxed' and 'engaged'. He also had more people showing up at his regular team meetings.

Paul enjoyed the writing exercise, and the original 15 minutes grew to 30 minutes or an hour. When I met him six months later, he had started a daily journal and extended his silence to include a walk in a local park.

Who knows where Paul will take his practice of silence? Every once in a while it could be beneficial for him to consider extending the period of time to a full day or even a weekend. Yes, really! If you ever get a chance to try it, I would strongly recommend it. There are many options available – if your home is the last place you can be silent, consider going on a retreat. See what happens. It can be a rich and rewarding experience, and it can also be a little scary. Either way, it is eye-opening.

Making space for silence can mean not talking, or avoiding noise. However, the kind of silence I want you to pursue is in moments between thoughts – where you do not actively distract yourself from silence. For Paul, writing a journal gave him a gradual introduction to silence. He had to walk before he could run. Think of it as a warm-up before serious exercise – when the muscles are ready, you can have a more beneficial workout without the risk of strain!

Not speaking is one way to get more comfortable with silence. Another way is to be more aware of how your body can help.

We also show our discomfort with silence through extraneous or distracting movement, which in most people creates unnecessary tension and fatigue in the body. It can also affect posture and general alignment.

 case study Maris: something in the way she moves

I met Maris for the first time as I tripped over her at the start of the Boston marathon. I was one of the slow runners, and she was one of the ones I didn't see again until the multiple sclerosis pasta party later that evening – she was so far ahead of me she would have had time to do the marathon again before I finished. We laughed that night at my gracefulness at the starting line and started talking about work and life generally. After a few minutes of discussion, I learned she was leading a start-up biotech firm and was now at a crucial stage of fund-raising. She asked if I would help her and her team on the initial public offering (IPO). Of course!

The IPO would entail many meetings with, and presentations to, potential investors and banks. The business was going public, with a broader array of shareholders and complex public governance. It would involve mainly tough audiences with short attention spans – people who made judgements fairly quickly as to the capability of the leadership team. Because of this, it was critical that everyone on the team, particularly the Leader/CEO, in this case Maris, came across as competent, strong, stable and focused.

As I got to know Maris over the course of a few meetings, I could see she would have a particular challenge on her plate. She never stopped moving. When she stood still, she was moving. When she sat down, she was moving. But as she was moving, it didn't always have a purpose or function. The movement was usually subtle and not always immediately perceptible. Standing still, she shifted her weight slightly from foot to foot. Sitting, she would often change her position or weight or tap her foot. There was always something in her hands – a pen, paper, some notes, a piece of wrapper she was twisting. When she did move to pick something up or do something, the movement never really 'finished' – she would move immediately to the next one. It felt constant. Like a water tap, you turn it on, you change the flow of water by adjusting the pressure, and then you stop it by turning the tap off. Maris moved without a clear start, change or stop to what she was doing.

The initial feedback we got from potential investors was that she was 'lightweight' and 'not focused'. 'Not likely to be able to handle the pressure.' 'Lacked gravitas.' If you knew Maris, you would understand that this was not true. But as I have said time and again throughout this book, impressions don't have to be right to matter. It was time to see if we could close the gap between the impression and the reality.

I discussed with Maris how she felt about this. She said she had been told since she was a child that she was active, energetic and dynamic, and saw it as an important part of her success. She believed people would think she was lazy or incapable if she didn't move. She felt that moving a lot made her appear on top of things. She was nonetheless unaware of how much she was moving, and actually thought of herself as a swan – calm and beautiful on top, but under the water paddling like hell! How could others see it so differently?

I did some exercises with her to see how she felt when she didn't move as much. Her discomfort was palpable, particularly if she had nothing in her hand or if she wasn't fidgeting or tapping her foot, or if she sat still for too long (meaning about 30 seconds). She referred to it as 'nothing happening'.

But not moving was the path to Maris's 'silence'. She needed to understand that 'nothing happening' gave the listeners a chance to absorb what she was saying, for insight to occur, for her to emphasise what was important and to demonstrate her power and strength.

Over the next few weeks, we practised several key exercises. Most of them involved her having to use less movement, which would focus more attention on her and her messages. This didn't mean not moving at all, just less – movement that was more focused and relevant.

Most people who use movement to mask a discomfort with silence share some characteristics. They tend to:

- shift, rock or lean into one or the other hip; they rarely have their weight on both feet at one time
- walk at uneven speeds: even short distances will combine a quick burst with stops and some meandering steps
- bump into furniture or doorways more often than the average person
- fidget, twitch, tap their foot, always have something in the hand (lots of twisted paper clips and sweet wrappers); they also fiddle with buttons or threads on clothing

- stand too close or too far away in social situations
- never appear to 'finish' the movement – tasks may get unfinished or items put back in the wrong place

Maris did get her finance, after some very hard work to persuade her investors that she could lead the company into the next stage of growth. By practising less, and more focused, movement, she stopped distracting her listeners and created a feeling of control and gravitas. She raised her awareness about how she used her body to confirm a personal belief about herself (active and dynamic means not lazy, and therefore desirable) and enabled her to decide that the way she moved wasn't serving her.

At the same time as getting her to cut down on the extraneous movement, I encouraged her to meditate. I suggested a simple technique that consisted of sitting quietly for several minutes, focusing on her breath, a word or phrase – she could also do this while standing or walking. She concentrated on inhaling, then changed gently to exhaling, and stopped. Then started again. This helped her become aware of what it was like to be still and where the tension was in her body. Over time, her urge to move was replaced by greater comfort, with 'nothing happening'.

There are many traditions and countless ways to practise meditation, and everyone needs to find what is right for them. If you are feeling better when you have finished, you are probably doing it right. It's no more complicated than that.

You can incorporate breathing, walking or writing into ways of beginning to practise silence. Most of us are not as extreme as Paul or Maris, but we can all benefit from more silence in our lives. Start in small ways to get a taste for it. Rather than going from morning to night without a break from distraction, steal a few moments in your everyday activity for silence.

My friend Holly, the mother of three small children, resists the temptation to collapse in front of the television after the children are asleep. She still flops on the sofa, but she leaves the TV off for at least 15 minutes, and sits quietly. She told me that just not turning on the TV immediately means that the urge to watch it disappears. Sometimes she finds after this moment of silence that she feels energised enough to pick up a book or give herself a pampering facial. Before children, she was a professional Cordon Bleu chef. By turning off the TV, she discovered she played around in the kitchen more. The time that would otherwise be spent watching a programme she had already seen, or surfing mindlessly through the many channels before realising that an hour had passed, was now spent doing something that made her feel good about herself. The biggest benefit she claims from introducing 15 minutes of silence is that she doesn't get the tension headaches that she used to get. She resists the temptation to be distracted, and opts for silence.

A friend of mine suffered a heart attack many years ago, and during his treatment he was given a stress monitor to wear under his shirt for a month, to determine which things in his daily life were stressing him the most. The results were surprising. The things he said he found most relaxing were actually the most taxing on his body. Driving was the biggest culprit, in particular being in traffic or stationary at red lights on the way to and from work. He took this information seriously and decided that since he couldn't stop driving, he would make an effort to be more aware of his stress levels. Now while he drives, he leaves the radio off and focuses on quiet, calm breathing at the lights and in traffic. The results over the last two weeks of the test have been dramatic. His heart rate is more regular and his blood pressure has dropped to more normal levels.

If, now and then, you can go alone to a café, just sit quietly and eat your meal or drink your coffee without a newspaper or book. See what happens. Don't be self-conscious about being alone. Someone said to me once that they felt silly sitting alone in a restaurant. The truth is that you think about yourself more than others do. Even the busiest places offer us an opportunity to practise silence. Remember, I want you to pursue moments between thoughts where you do not actively distract yourself from silence.

Another technique for becoming more comfortable with silence is as you go about your everyday activity, stop when you can and ask yourself, 'What part of me is resting?' By doing this, like my friend at the red traffic light, you can start to observe your unique physical state and create a conscious moment of rest or silence. Rest assured, there is always a part of you that is resting.

It is my hope that you will develop comfort with silence by practising it using the suggestions in this book. If you think about it, silence is where you can really get something from nothing! Remember that silence is not just the absence of noise, but being still or at rest. Enjoy.

afterword

We are all faced with boulders of various shapes and sizes throughout our lives. In my experience, and that of my clients, communication offers a path that can be used to walk around some of the most troublesome or seemingly insurmountable boulders.

It's never easy to effect changes in habits, especially when they have been ingrained over many years. The first step is always recognising what needs to change and then taking responsibility for it.

I'm grateful you have spent time here. I hope you have found something useful for yourself in this book and can use it as a guide to behaving your way into the changes you want to see.

further reading

The following is a shortlist of books that have proved helpful to me and/or my clients: some my clients have told me about, others I have recommended to them; many sit with pride of place on my desk as loyal sources of inspiration and reference.

Stephan Bodian *Meditation for Dummies* John Wiley 2006

Tony Buzan *How to Mind Map: the ultimate thinking tool that will change your life* HarperCollins 2002

Mihaly Csikszentmihaly *Finding Flow* Basic Books 1997

Wayne Dyer *The Power of Intention* Hay House 2004

Juliet Erickson *The Art of Persuasion* Hodder & Stoughton 2004

Moshe Feldenkrais *The Elusive Obvious* Meta Publications 1989

— *Awareness through Movement* HarperCollins 1991

Judee Gee *Intuition: awakening your inner guide* Samuel Weiser 1999

Daniel Goleman *Emotional Intelligence* HarperCollins 2004

Lynn Grabhorn *Excuse Me, Your Life is Waiting* Hodder & Stoughton 2005

John Gray *How to Get What You Want in the Workplace* Ebury 2003

Thich Nhat Hanh *Peace Is Every Step: the path of mindfulness in everyday life* Random House 1991

Sue Knight *NLP at Work* Nicholas Brealey 2002

Gary Kraftsow *Yoga for Wellness* Arkana 1999

— *Yoga for Transformation* Arkana 2002

Robert MacDonald & Caro Ness *Alexander Technique* Dorling Kindersley 2001

Joseph O'Connor & Ian McDermott *Principles of NLP* HarperCollins 1996

Lynne Robinson, Helge Fisher, Jacqueline Knox & Gordon Thomson *The Official Body Control Pilates Manual* Macmillan, new edition 2002

Don Miguel Ruiz *The Four Agreements: a practical guide to personal freedom* Amber-Allen 2001

Susan Scott *Fierce Conversations: achieving success in work and in life, one conversation at a time* Piatkus 2003

Twyla Tharp *The Creative Habit: learn it and use it for life* Simon & Schuster 2003

Eckhart Tolle *The Power of Now: a guide to spiritual enlightenment* Namaste 1997

— *Stillness Speaks* Hodder & Stoughton 2003

Barbara Winter *Making a Living Without a Job: winning ways for creating work that you love* Bantam 1993

index